Catholic Shrines and Places of Pilgrimage in the United States

NATIONAL CONFERENCE OF CATHOLIC BISHOPS

In March 1989, the bishops' Committee on Migration authorized the preparation of a Catholic directory of shrines and places of pilgrimage in the United States. The Office for the Pastoral Care of Migrants and Refugees was commissioned to prepare this publication for the promotion of the Shrine and Pilgrimage Apostolate. This Jubilee edition of the directory, *Catholic Shrines and Places of Pilgrimage in the United States*, has been compiled and updated under the leadership of Most Rev. James P. Keleher, archbishop of Kansas City in Kansas and the episcopal liaison for the Shrine and Pilgrimage Apostolate. It is hereby authorized for publication by the undersigned.

Monsignor Dennis M. Schnurr
General Secretary
NCCB/USCC

ISBN 1-57455-158-2

First Printing, January 1998
Second Printing, March 2000

The Jubilee Year 2000 logo is trademarked by the United States Catholic Conference (USCC) and may not be used in any way without the prior written permission of the USCC. Permission may be requested by writing the Secretariat for the Third Millennium and Jubilee Year 2000, 3211 Fourth Street, N.E., Washington, DC 20017.

Contents

Introduction

Dear Friends,

The Ad Hoc Committee on Shrines is pleased to present the Jubilee edition of the directory on *Catholic Shrines and Places of Pilgrimage in the United States*. This revised millennium edition contains new information on many shrines and their pastoral activities. I am encouraged that the Pilgrimage Apostolate is gaining its rightful place in the pastoral programs in our country.

For centuries, shrines throughout the world have been centers of devotional life for the faithful. Here in the United States, dioceses and parishes are becoming increasingly aware of the quality of pastoral programs offered at shrines. Within the episcopal conferences of various countries, special offices for shrines and pilgrimages have been established and many dioceses have appointed pilgrimage directors to coordinate the pilgrimage movement. In the United States, the pilgrimage movement received new impetus with the establishment of the National Organization of Shrines and Pilgrimage Apostolate (NASPA).

The work of the Ad Hoc Committee on Shrines with Archbishop Francis George, Archbishop Charles Chaput, Archbishop John Vlazny, Bishop John Meyers, Bishop Sean O'Malley, and Rev. Msgr. Anthony Czarnecki, consultor, has had a positive impact on the growth and development of the Pilgrimage Apostolate. I also want to recognize the cooperation of the Catholic bishops' Secretariat for the Third Millennium and the Jubilee Year 2000 for their support in making pilgrimages an integral part of the celebration of the Year 2000. Finally, I am grateful to the shrine directors for their assistance in preparing this directory.

May this Jubilee edition of the directory on *Catholic Shrines and Places of Pilgrimage* motivate and inspire the faithful to rediscover fuller spiritual life by undertaking a pilgrimage to a sacred shrine and, like the disciples on the road to Emmaus, may they meet Jesus on the journey.

With every best wish I remain,
Sincerely yours in Christ,

+James P. Keleher

Most Reverend James Patrick Keleher
Archbishop of Kansas City in Kansas
Chairman of the Committee on Shrines

Preface

A pilgrimage to the Holy Land to visit the places sanctified by the life and death of Jesus Christ or a trip to Rome to witness the life of the early Church leaves us with an unforgettable memory. The pilgrimage trail to these and other shrines throughout the world is crowded with people from various walks of life in search of spiritual benefits and supernatural values. Although in our country the word *pilgrimage* is not as yet part of our daily vocabulary, nevertheless, with the renewed interest in religion, pilgrimages have made inroads into the spiritual life of the faithful.

A pilgrimage has ancient roots, biblical significance, and a long tradition in the Church. It is a spiritual journey for religious motives to a holy site where the grace of God is manifested in a special way. Abraham, our Father in Faith, was called to leave his familiar surroundings and go to an unknown destination, the land of Canaan. On his pilgrimage, he encountered the presence of God, which enriched his life. Jesus Christ also followed the tradition of his forefathers and participated in a pilgrimage to the temple in Jerusalem. Many disciples whom he called left everything and became pilgrims; in the dusty roads of Palestine they recognized Jesus as the Messiah and rediscovered the true meaning of life.

In our contemporary living, we often feel crushed by the demands of the day and are so caught up in our daily routine that the path of life seems continually to wind back on itself in a spiral course through the uncertainties and anxieties of life. Other times, we feel discouraged and burnt out; the road of life seems to coil through difficulties, loneliness, and meaningless existence. In such situations, a pilgrimage can make a difference and help us to redirect our life, replenish our spiritual energy, rediscover our goals, enrich our life of faith, strengthen the bond of love and friendship with our family and community, but above all, experience the healing power of Jesus Christ.

To be on a pilgrimage means to be ever open to a new beginning, to a new vision of life that leads into new tomorrows, no matter how uncertain or difficult. A pilgrimage allows us to dream a new dream, to experience a new joy that only God can offer. A pilgrimage provides many opportunities for sacrifices and allows us to accept inconveniences and crosses with the common belief that our sacrifices become the seed of a new tree of life. Life is indeed a journey and a road that leads to God. As we walk through a pilgrimage we do not walk alone. He who came to share our destiny joins us in new future walks.

When we reach our destination—the sacred site—we feel welcomed by God, immersed in his forgiving love and mercy. The atmosphere of the shrine inspires spontaneous reflection and prayer. We return home changed, like Moses returned from the Holy Mountain, where he conversed with God. Though the reality of life may not change, our outlook on life is transformed. Very often people visit the shrines as tourists but leave as pilgrims. The atmosphere of prayer, the availability of the sacraments of Penance and Eucharist, and the pastoral services of a given shrine lead many pilgrims onto the road of conversion as they experience the healing power of Jesus Christ. The Holy Father has referred many times to shrines as places of new evangelization. On the occasion celebrating seven hundred years of the Loreto shrine, Pope John Paul II stated, "the effectiveness of shrines is increasingly measured by their capacity to respond to the growing need felt by human beings in the frantic pace of modern life for silent, thoughtful contact with God and with themselves." The shrines, indeed, create an environment where we feel spiritually rejuvenated in the atmosphere of peace, reflection, and prayer. In his apostolic letter *Tertio Millennio Adveniente*, the Holy Father invites all Christians to prepare for the Great Jubilee Year with "eyes of faith" turned to our own century, searching for whatever bears witness not only to our history but also to God's intervention in human affairs. As we approach the Year 2000, we should consider a pilgrimage journey as a part of the process of rediscovery of our own particular mission in life and in the life of the Church.

At a time when secularistic culture makes every effort to reduce a human person to a mere commodity, to be exploited, wasted, or used for personal gain, the shrines become beacons of hope and new life. In a society where hate, revenge, and selfishness seem to be a way of life, the shrines proclaim forgiveness, love, and sacrifice in service to others. Every shrine is a place of conversion and a new beginning where God extends his merciful hand and provides new grace and new strength to fulfill our destiny on the pilgrimage of life.

May this directory on shrines serve as an important resource to help you and guide you to find the holy site where you may experience divine mercy, love, and forgiveness.

Msgr. Anthony Czarnecki

Rev. Msgr. Anthony Czarnecki
USCC Consultant
Shrine and Pilgrimage Apostolate

Shrines, Pilgrimages, and the Great Jubilee of the Year 2000

As the Third Millennium of the Redemption draws near, God is preparing a great springtime for Christianity, and, we can already see its first signs (*Redemptoris Missio*, 86).

On December 24, 1999, Pope John Paul II will open the Holy Year door in St. Peter's Bascilica and inaugurate the Great Jubilee of the Year 2000. A Jubilee that commemorates the fact that the coming of Jesus Christ as a tiny child in the womb of a young Jewish woman and his birth in Bethlehem two thousand years ago propelled world history irreversibly.

Our preparation is, above all, a three-year pilgrimage toward the celebration of the Great Jubilee of the Year 2000. Like all pilgrimages, it is primarily an opportunity to deepen our spiritual lives and become holy people. We begin this journey of faith by focusing on the destination: Life with Jesus Christ. This pilgrimage of years becomes a time of self-examination, expectation, and intense prayer; it is likened to an advent season of hope, rooted in the presence of the Holy Spirit (*Tertio Millennio Adveniente* [TMA], cf. 20). During this time we not only examine what changes need to be made, but we also celebrate the good already present in our own lives, in the Church, and in our world—though often hidden from our eyes (cf. TMA, 46).

The guideposts for this great pilgrimage are the papal exhortation *Tertio Millennio Adveniente* (*On the Coming of the Third Millennium*, 1994), the rich biblical tradition of "Jubilee," and the renewed study and application of the teachings of the Second Vatican Council. We begin by proclaiming that Jesus Christ is our Savior and Redeemer and therefore we seek to deepen our relationship with Jesus Christ, the fulfillment of Jubilee (see Lk 4:19). Secondly, we seek to examine our conscience in light of the Gospel and the teachings of the Church. This provides us an opportunity for repentance, forgiveness, and reconciliation—to enter the new millennium as a new people. A people who are healed by the love of Jesus Christ and strengthened by the power of the holy Spirit. In Jesus Christ we see that the "joy of every Jubilee is, above all, a joy based on the forgiveness of sins, the joy of conversion . . . the precondition for reconciliation with God on the part of both individuals and communities" (TMA, 32). These last years of the twentieth century are an opportunity to be on a pilgrimage into the twenty-first century, where we undertake a pilgrimage to reconfirm our faith, sustain our hope, and rekindle our charity (cf. TMA, 31).

The bishops' Subcommittee on the Third Millennium suggests several pastoral planning principles for our pilgrimage to celebrate the Great Jubilee and enter into the twenty-first century. These can be considered as guideposts for the three years of preparation.

1. Take a time out! Reflect. Begin with a fresh start (let the land lie fallow).

In order to prepare ourselves for the Great Jubilee we need to take a break from the "busy-ness" of contemporary life. Our home, work, and church lives are incredibly busy today—typically marked by endless activities that provide little time for personal reflection or spiritual growth. The next few years provide us an opportunity to slow down in order to acquire insight as we move into the Third Millennium. Pilgrimages can be an excellent opportunity for this personal reflection.

2. Study the Scriptures and the teachings of the Church.

Pilgrimages can provide an opportunity for pilgrims to learn more about their faith through theological reflection and reading the Scriptures. Themes during the pilgrimage can center on the four constitutions of Vatican II, the Holy Father's exhortation *Tertio Millennio Adveniente*, and other recent teachings. Use the *Catechism of the Catholic Church* as a resource for this study and reflection.

3. Keep the vision focused on spiritual growth rather than programs.

The Holy Father is inviting us to use these years of preparation as an opportunity to deepen our spiritual lives, to continue our task of being holy people. How does the organization of the pilgrimage further this goal of helping people become holy women and men?

4. Bring people together to collaborate and to be inclusive.

The call to Jubilee is an invitation to the whole Church and must involve the collaboration of many different people and ministries. In planning pilgrimages, remember to involve representatives from the various ministries of the Church. The diocesan contact person for the Third Millennium should be aware of all that is happening, and pilgrimages should be considered as part of the diocesan effort to prepare for and celebrate the Jubilee Year.

5. Create enthusiasm and a hopeful attitude for the message of Jesus Christ while acknowledging the good that is already happening in our church communities.

Our passion and zeal for the Gospel and our belief in God's presence within human history give us energy and sustain our hope. We have reason to hope because of the presence of the Holy Spirit in the world today. It has been said that people with hope live with an eye toward the future; they seek to build up rather than maintain or tear down. We are a Church with many rich blessings and ministries. We must build on the good things present in contemporary church life today.

6. Work ecumenically whenever possible.

The Jubilee Year is not solely a "Catholic" moment but a Christian celebration to remember the great things that have taken place because of Christ's birth and the presence of Christianity in world history. A Jubilee pilgrimage can be an opportunity for all men and women of faith to come together to reflect on the presence of Jesus Christ in our lives these past years and to seek forgiveness for those times when we have not been faithful to the Gospel.

7. Infuse the themes of Jubilee into present church life.

Use the themes of 1997–1999 to provide a focus for pilgrimages. Develop a connection among the liturgical year, the theme of the pilgrimage, and the Jubilee. Build on what is already present rather than attempting to recreate the wheel.

8. Celebrate Jubilee!

In the year 2000, we celebrate two thousand years of Christ's presence in human history—what more do we have to say! Use these next few years to prepare properly to celebrate the Jubilee Year. Identify what changes need to be made personally, as a faith community, and as society. Be reconciled with Christ and work to stand in solidarity with all humanity so that as the dawn of the new millennium approaches we can truly rest and celebrate that we are ready to open the door to a new milennium of Christianity. Pilgrimages during the Jubilee Year should also have this element of praise and thanksgiving for Christ's presence in our lives.

Paul K Henderson

Mr. Paul Henderson
Executive Director
Secretariat for the Third Millennium
and the Jubilee Year 2000

A Vision for the Journey:
"Open Wide
the Doors to Christ"

INTRODUCTION

The U.S. bishops, in their document *Called and Gifted for the Third Millennium*, begin their reflection by asking, "What is the Spirit saying to the world today through the Church in the United States, particularly through the lives of lay men and women?" We echo this question by asking: What is the Spirit saying to us today as we approach this unique historical time, this *kairos* moment, of the Great Jubilee of the Year 2000 and the crossing into the Third Millennium?

Pope John Paul II, in the beginning of his apostolic exhortation *Tertio Millennio Adveniente* (*On the Coming of the Third Millennium*) provides a glimpse to the answer. He says, "As the Third Millennium of the new era draws near, our thoughts turn spontaneously to the words of the Apostle Paul: 'When the fullness of time had come, God sent forth his Son, born of woman'" (Gal 4:4) (TMA, 1). The whole Church is invited, through three years of preparation, to open the door to the Third Millennium by opening the doors of our hearts to Jesus Christ, the second person of the Trinity. Therefore, this preparation is primarily a journey to deepen one's spiritual life—to be the holy people God calls us to be.

Being a holy person "requires effort and commitment to live the beatitudes" daily in our lives (*Called and Gifted for the Third Millennium*, p. 3) and to undertake repentance and forgiveness. It means practicing the theological virtues of faith, hope, and charity and the natural virtues of patience, courtesy, courage, and humility (Archbishop Daniel Buechlein, OSB, "Spirituality for the Year 2001," *Origins*, 27:2, May 29, 1997, p. 31). It means understanding the call to holiness as a gift from the Holy Spirit and our response as a gift to the Church and to the world (cf. *Called and Gifted*, p. 4).

An image we invite you to embrace for this journey is "Open Wide the Doors to Christ." When we open the doors of our hearts to Christ we seek a relationship with Jesus Christ, who is the way, the truth, and the life (cf. Jn 14:6). This image calls us to action and speaks of what we need to do and how we should respond to God's gift of love if we are to be holy. The image invites us, as Jesus himself did, to make the words of the prophet Isaiah our own: "The spirit of the Lord is upon me, because he has anointed me to bring good news to the poor. He has sent me to proclaim liberty to captives, recovery of sight to the blind, to let the oppressed go free, to proclaim a year of favor from the Lord" (Is 61:1–2).

Doors are a powerful symbol that evoke strong images. Open doors speak of welcome, hospitality, openness; closed doors convey isolation, discrimination, being shut out from community and love. The Incarnation itself is a powerful image whereby God opened the doors to the kingdom through the life, death, and resurrection of his son, Jesus Christ. Practicing Jubilee is a way to open the door to the Third Millennium since Jubilee offers concrete ways to live out one's faith in God (Maria Harris, *Proclaim Jubilee: A Spirituality for the Twenty-first Century*, John Knox/ Westminister Press). Jubilee shows us how to respond to God through Jesus Christ.

Our goal for these years is to open the door to the Year 2000 by celebrating Jubilee. Therefore, we propose an image of four doors to pass through in order to reach the Great Jubilee and the new millennium. First we open the door to Jesus Christ. Once we have passed through this door our hearts are opened to pass through the doors of repentance and conversion, community and unity, and justice and peace.

OPEN WIDE THE DOORS THROUGH JESUS CHRIST

The preparation for the Third Millennium provides us with a privileged historical opportunity—to proclaim anew to the world a profound faith that in Christ the Lord "can be found the key, the focal point, and the goal of all human history" (*Gaudium et Spes*, 10). We are invited to renew and deepen our faith in God by deepening our relationship with Jesus Christ: A relationship sustained and nurtured through the presence of the Holy Spirit in our world today.

These preparations provide us with the opportunity to usher in a "new evangelization" of holiness and service. "God is opening before the Church the horizons of a humanity more fully prepared for the sowing of the Gospel. . . . the moment has come to commit all of the Church's energies to a new evangelization. . . . No believer in Christ, no institution of the Church can avoid this supreme duty: To proclaim Christ to all peoples" (*Redemptoris Missio*, 3).

OPEN WIDE THE DOORS THROUGH PERSONAL CONVERSION
AND RECONCILIATION

To deepen one's spiritual life, Pope John Paul II invites the Church to enter into a kind of worldwide retreat, an intense period of prayer, a "journey of authentic conversion." This begins with an examination of conscience—the personal space and time to pause and be quiet, to listen to God speaking to us, an opportunity to let the land of our own lives lie fallow for a time. The "joy of every Jubilee is above all a joy based upon the forgiveness of sins, the joy of conversion" which "takes place in the heart of each person, extends to the believing community, and then reaches to the whole of humanity" (TMA, 32). This spirit of repentance and conversion leads us to be people of reconciliation. We, individually and as a Church, are also called in a spirit of penance to ask God's forgiveness for those times in our history when we have fallen far short of serving his kingdom through our own negligence and sin (TMA, 33).

OPEN WIDE THE DOORS THROUGH COMMUNITY AND UNITY

This journey also calls us to examine how we participate in the community of believers, and to look, in a special way, at how we have been instruments of Christian unity: to restore the bonds of faith between Christians and even among Catholic communities. We are called to community through our baptism, where we become sons and daughters of God. We are all God's children and belong to God. It is through this community that we are enriched in faith and grow in the knowledge and love of God. And, it is the family that is the first community to which we belong, the domestic Church.

A significant goal in *Tertio Millennio Adveniente* is Christian unity. How can we embrace the pope's wishes to "celebrate the Great Jubilee, if not completely united, at least much closer to overcoming the divisions of the second millennium . . . "? "It is essential to not only continue along the path of dialogue on doctrinal matters, but above all to be more committed to prayer for Christian unity" (TMA, 34). Let us work to further Christian unity, realizing that this "unity is a gift of the Holy Spirit" (TMA, 34). Consider our ecumenical prayer to be that which Our Lord taught us, "Our Father, who art in heaven . . . " It is important to remember that that which unites us, Jesus Christ, is far greater than anything that divides us.

OPEN WIDE THE DOORS BY PRACTICING JUSTICE

The Great Jubilee of the Year 2000, should be seen as a season of the Lord's favor (Lk 4:18–19, Is 61:2, Lv 25:10), in which "the presence of the Holy Spirit will be more deeply experienced, impelling Christians to preach the Gospel with new power, giving hope of liberation to the marginalized and the oppressed" (Avery Dulles, "John Paul II and the Advent of the New Millennium," America, 173:19 [1995], p. 11). Jesus, the evangelizer, is anointed by the Spirit of the Lord to proclaim Good News to the poor and to everyone a year of jubilee—a time of freedom from bondage, restoration, forgiveness of debts, and favor from the Lord (cf. Lv 25:8 ff).

Today, we are called to imitate the great followers of Christ who have cooperated with God's grace in the transformation of the world in such social justice movements as the abolition of slavery and the death penalty; the promotion of civil rights, the rights of workers, and women's rights; the expansion of higher education opportunities; and respect for life from conception to natural death. The jubilee tradition reminds us that all the earth is God's and we are stewards of that earth. Being "jubilee" people, we must not be afraid "to build in the next century a civilization worthy of the human person, a true culture of freedom . . . . In doing so, we shall see that the tears of this century have prepared the ground of a new springtime of the human spirit" (John Paul II, Address to the United Nations, Oct. 5, 1995, no. 18).

MARY, THE MODEL OF FAITH AND HOPE
FOR THE TWENTY-FIRST CENTURY

Earlier we spoke of these years as likened to an extended Advent season. Mary is the primary patroness of this new Advent. Just as the Blessed Virgin carried the Christ child in her womb before his birth, "so the present millennium, in its final years, bears within itself the seeds of the millennium now waiting to be born" (Avery Dulles, "John Paul II and the Advent of the New Millennium," America,173:19 [1995] p. 10).

Mary, in fact, constantly points to her Divine Son. She is for all believers the model of faith which is put into practice (TMA, 43). Mary is "a woman of hope" who gives "full expression to the longing of the poor of Yahweh and is a radiant model for those who entrust themselves with all their hearts to the promises of God" (TMA, 48). Mary becomes for us the "perfect model of love toward both God and neighbor" (TMA, 54).

THE JOURNEY: GUIDED BY VATICAN II AND
THE CATECHISM OF THE CATHOLIC CHURCH

As a Catholic Church, we are compelled to examine our conscience according to the renewal challenges of the Second Vatican Council, the "Advent Liturgy" for the Great Jubilee of the Year 2000. The best preparation for the Jubilee Year will be a "renewed commitment to apply, as faithfully as possible, the teachings of Vatican II to the life of every individual and of the whole Church" (TMA, 20). We are challenged to strengthen our commitment to deeper pursuit of holiness, wider community participation, and a stronger witness of faith. Aided by the Catechism of the Catholic Church (TMA, 42), we are invited to grow in our Catholic identity and knowledge of and enthusiasm for the faith. Through prayer and dialogue, we are to seek deeper unity within the Catholic family and to continue our ecumenical pursuit of full communion with fellow Christians.

Paul K Henderson

Mr. Paul Henderson
Executive Director
Secretariat for the Third Millennium
and the Jubilee Year 2000

Midwest

National Shrine of
Our Lady of the Snows

DIOCESE OF BELLEVILLE
442 S. DEMAZENOD DRIVE • BELLEVILLE, IL 62223 • (618) 397-6700 • FAX (618) 398-6549

HISTORY OF THE SHRINE

In 1818, Saint Eugene DeMazenod, the founder of the Missionary Oblates of Mary Immaculate, accepted the care and ministry of the Shrine of Notre Dame de Laus in France for his newly established group of missionaries. Thus, Oblates have been linked to shrine ministry from the time of their founding. The Missionary Oblates of Mary Immaculate, the order of priests and brothers who operate the shrine, have always called upon Mary as their principal patroness.

Devotion to Mary under the title of Our Lady of the Snows has some ties to a legend of a snowfall in Rome in AD 352. In a dream, Mary had indicated to a Roman couple where she wanted a church built in her honor. However, Our Lady of the Snows is honored here, not so much because of the legend, but because of her special role in a Church that is, by its very nature, missionary. In 1941, Fr. Paul Schulte, OMI, a missionary in the Arctic regions of Canada, introduced the devotion to Mary under that title to those in the Midwest. Wishing to encourage members of the Missionary Association of Mary Immaculate to pray for and to become involved in missionary activity of the Oblates, Fr. Edwin J. Guild, OMI, founded the shrine at St. Henry's Seminary in Belleville. In 1958, the shrine was moved to its present location on more than 200 acres of beautifully landscaped gardens and devotional areas. It is considered the largest oudoor shrine in North America.

Devotional areas include the main shrine (outdoor altar and 2,400-seat amphitheater, Christ the King Chapel, Mary Chapel, and Rosary Courts), the Way of the Cross, Agony in the Garden, Resurrection Garden, Annunciation Garden, Lourdes Grotto, Mother's and Father's Prayer Walk, the Edwin J. Guild Center, and the Church of Our Lady of the Snows.

The shrine is open every day to people of all faiths and denominations. Annual events include the Easter and Egg Display, Our Lady of Snows Healing Novena, Polish-American Celebration, Youth Sing Praise, and World Youth Day. The Way of Lights Christmas Celebration starts the Friday before Thanksgiving and ends the Sunday after New Year's Day.

In preparation for the Jubilee Year 2000, the shrine has erected a Millennium electro-art sculpture depicting 1997 Year of Faith. The theme is "Christ, the Light of the World." Similar sculptures will be added each year representing 1998 Year of Hope, 1999 Year of Love, and 2000 Year of Renewal. The events throughout each year will follow the theme of that year. Some of the programs to be held in preparation of the Millennium are Earth Day Celebration, Ecumenical Days of Reflection, Family Bible Week, Global Walk for Jesus, a Millennium Renaissance Fair for Families, Millennium Video, and Nine-month Novena prior to January 2000. On New Year's Eve 1999, the shrine will host a special spiritual celebration welcoming the Third Millennium. It will include an evening banquet, a paraliturgical service from 11:00 p.m. to midnight, and guest accommodations at the Shrine Motel.

SCHEDULE OF MASSES
Sunday Vigil: 5:00 p.m.
Sunday: 9:30 a.m., 11:30 a.m.
Daily: April–October, 7:30 a.m., 11:30 a.m., 5:00 p.m.; November–March,
    7:30 a.m., 11:30 a.m.
Confessions: 30 minutes before each Mass

DEVOTIONS
Rosary: Lourdes Grotto, April 1–October 31, Monday–Friday, 8:45 a.m.;
    Saturday, 8:30 p.m.

FACILITIES
Visitors Center
Gift Shop
Full Service Restaurant
Shrine Motel, 78 rooms (AAA)

OTHER
Pilgrimage season: April 1–October 31. Free guided tours available on an open air
Tram (weather permitting): Monday–Saturday, 9:30 a.m., 12:30 p.m., 2:30 p.m.;
    Sunday, 12:30 p.m., 2:30 p.m.

Dominican Shrine of St. Jude Thaddeus

ARCHDIOCESE OF CHICAGO
1909 S. ASHLAND AVENUE • CHICAGO, IL 60608• (312) 226-0020

HISTORY OF THE SHRINE

The Dominican Shrine of St. Jude Thaddeus, opened in October 1929, encompasses a ministry of preaching, spiritual direction, and a network of people at prayer—The Friends of St. Jude. The Friends of St. Jude write, telephone, and stop at the shrine to request prayers for their special needs. The shrine, in the parish church of St. Pius V, is staffed by the Dominican Fathers and Brothers of the Province of St. Albert the Great.

SCHEDULE OF MASSES

Sunday Parish Masses: 8:00 a.m., 11:15 a.m. (English); 9:30 a.m., 1:00 p.m.,
    4:30 p.m. (Spanish)
Holy Day of Obligation: 8:00 a.m. (parish), noon (shrine service)
Confessions: Saturday, 5:00 p.m.; Thursday and each novena day, noon, 6:25 p.m.

DEVOTIONS

Rosary, novena prayers, and eucharist each day (except Sunday) at noon;
    Thursday at 6:30 p.m.
Solemn novenas are held five times a year (January, March, May, July, and October),
    with services at 9:50 a.m., noon, and 6:30 p.m. (also Sunday at 11:00 a.m.).

FACILITIES

Gift Shop

National Shrine of St. Anne

ARCHDIOCESE OF CHICAGO
2751 W. 38 PLACE • CHICAGO, IL 60632-1686 • (773) 927-2421

HISTORY OF THE SHRINE

 In 1900, the Rev. Cyril A. Poissant sought the permission of Archbishop Patrick Fehan to install a shrine in honor of Saint Anne in his church. Most of his parishioners were French Canadian immigrants—with a strong devotion to St. Anne de Beaupre. Unable to travel to their homeland for the annual novena to their patroness, the parish priest began the Novena in Honor of Saint Anne de Brighton with a tiny relic he had in his possession. It was the first shrine in the city of Chicago.

Because of the many spiritual favors and miracles of grace, the shrine received a larger relic of Saint Anne from Apt, France, making it the largest relic of the saint in the United States. Over the years, thousands of pilgrims have attended the annual Novena held here each year from July 18 to 26, the Feast of Saint Anne. The Centennial Celebration of the founding of the shrine will be held in July 2000.

Membership in the Archconfraternity of Saint Anne offers remembrance in a Novena of Masses each month throughout the year. Those wishing to enroll in the Archconfraternity are invited to write to the shrine at the above address.

SCHEDULE OF MASSES
During Novena Week Daily: 6:30 a.m., 9:30 a.m.
Novena Mass: Weekdays, 9:30 a.m.; Sunday, 10:30 a.m.
Confessions: Before the 9:30 a.m. Mass and after all Novena Services

DEVOTIONS
During Novena Week Morning Prayers: Daily: After 9:30 a.m. Mass
Afternoon Novena Service: Daily, 2:00 p.m.; Sunday, 4:00 p.m.
Evening Novena Service: Daily, 7:00 p.m.
Veneration of Relic: After each service
Blessing for Children: Saturday, 2:00 p.m.
Blessing of the Sick: Sunday, 4:00 p.m.
Outdoor Procession: July 20, 23, and 26, after evening service

FACILITIES
Cafeteria
Religious Goods Store

National Shrine of St. Jude

ARCHDIOCESE OF CHICAGO
3200 E. 91ST STREET • CHICAGO, IL 60617 • (312) 236-7782
MAILING ADDRESS: 205 W. MONROE STREET • CHICAGO, IL 60606

HISTORY OF THE SHRINE

Devotion to St. Jude, one of the Twelve Apostles and a cousin of Jesus, was slow to develop, perhaps due to confusion of his name with that of Judas Iscariot. Impetus to this devotion was given by the Lord himself who, in a vision, directed St. Bridget of Sweden to turn to St. Jude with faith and confidence.

The first widespread public veneration of St. Jude in the western hemisphere took place in 1911 in Chile at a large shrine to the apostle built by the Claretian Missionary Fathers. In the United States, the first major shrine to the apostle was established in 1929 in Chicago, also by the Claretian Missionary Fathers. The National Shrine of St. Jude contains the largest first-class relic of the saint in North America.

During the Great Depression, Fr. James Tort, CMF, began a Novena to St. Jude, the patron saint of difficult or hopeless cases, on February 17, 1929. The congregation responded enthusiastically and spread the word of the devotions across the nation. Over the years, many other shrines and publications devoted to St. Jude have come into being. He is a model of Christ's disciples to all who honor him.

The shrine has received more than one million letters of thanks for favors granted through the intercession of St. Jude. The shrine is open to the public 7:00 a.m.–8:00 p.m. daily.

SCHEDULE OF MASSES

Sunday Vigil: 7:00 p.m.
Sunday: 10:15 a.m., 4:30 p.m. (English); 7:15 a.m., 8:45 a.m., 11:45 a.m., 1:15 p.m., 6:00 p.m. (Spanish)
Weekday: 8:15 a.m. (English), 7:00 a.m., 7:00 p.m. (Spanish)
Holy Day of Obligation: 8:15 a.m., 4:30 p.m. (English); 7:00 a.m., 7:00 p.m. (Spanish)
Confessions: Saturday: 3:00–5:00 p.m., 6:00–7:00 p.m.

DEVOTIONS

St. Jude: Wednesday, 5:30 p.m., 8:00 p.m.
Solemn Novenas to St. Jude:
>February (preceding Lent),
>April (preceding Mother's Day),
>June (preceding Father's Day),
>August and October (Feast of St. Jude)

Solemn Novena Services: Monday–Saturday, 2:00 p.m., 5:30 p.m., 8:00 p.m.;
>Sunday, 3:00 p.m., 8:00 p.m.

FACILITIES

Gift Shop

LANGUAGES

English and Spanish

Our Lady of Pompeii Shrine

ARCHDIOCESE OF CHICAGO
1224 W. LEXINGTON STREET • CHICAGO, IL 60607 • (312) 421-3757

HISTORY OF THE SHRINE

In 1911, Our Lady of Pompeii Parish opened its arms to the wave of Italian immigrants who settled on the Near West Side of Chicago. From that day forward, the parish was a beacon and a comfort to all who sought refuge within its loving embrace. In 1923, ground was broken for the magnificent church we see today, resplendent with all its statues, original artwork, and marble. On October 10, 1994, the late and beloved Cardinal Joseph Bernardin proclaimed Our Lady of Pompeii Church a shrine dedicated to honor Mary, the Mother of God, because of its rich history within the Italian community. Its goal was once again to draw those of Italian heritage to itself and create a place of refuge in the city. The shrine is a center of spiritual and cultural growth for *all* who seek a deeper and richer experience of our faith and culture.

All pilgrims are welcomed to the shrine, where they will find a place of witness to the importance and centrality of prayer in their lives and will have an opportunity to deepen their commitment to God and devotion to Our Lady. The shrine provides a peaceful atmosphere where visitors get in touch with the message of Mary. Through individual and group pilgrimages, special prayer services, and other programs, visitors take time away from the world's anxieties, and when their shrine visit is over, return home refreshed and filled with a renewed sense of purpose to their lives.

Our Lady of Pompeii Shrine is only the second church in the world to house a *un ex-omnibus* relic of Blessed Grimoaldo Santamaria. He was a young Passionist seminarian who had a great devotion to the Blessed Mother and the Immaculate Conception at the time of his death in 1902. The shrine is the Midwest Center for the cause of canonization of this dedicated man, whom the pope declared "Blessed" after Grimoaldo's first miracle was approved July 2, 1994. His feast day is May 4.

SCHEDULE OF MASSES
Sunday: 8:30 a.m., 11:00 a.m.
Monday–Saturday: 7:30 a.m.

PRIVATE VISITATION
Monday–Friday: 9:00 a.m.–5:00 p.m.

DEVOTIONS

Healing Services: First Wednesday of each month, 7:00 p.m.
Pathways of Prayer: Third Wednesday of each month, 7:00 p.m.

FACILITIES

Shrine
Courtyard Fountain
Gift Shop

LANGUAGES

English and Italian

Our Lady of Sorrows Basilica The National Shrine of St. Peregrine

ARCHDIOCESE OF CHICAGO
3121 W. JACKSON BOULEVARD • CHICAGO, IL 60612 • (773) 638-5800

HISTORY OF THE SHRINE

Our Lady of Sorrows Parish was established in 1874 by the Servants of Mary (Servites), a religious order founded in the thirteenth century by seven Florentine merchants (The Seven Holy Founders). The first Servites arrived in the United States in 1870 and brought with them a devotion to the sorrows of Mary, a devotion that had become characteristic of Servites.

The cornerstone of the present Italian Renaissance-style church was laid in 1890, and the completed church was dedicated in 1902. The great coffered barrel-vaulted ceiling rises almost 80 feet above the white marble floor. The ceiling consists of 1,100 separate gold panels. The basilica has a majestic marble main altar and two major altars in the transepts. There are also ten smaller chapels in the basilica, five on either side of the nave. Surrounding the sanctuary are the sacristy, a shrine featuring a full-sized marble replica of Michelangelo's Pieta, and a choir chapel featuring fine oak paneling and choir stalls. The basilica seats 1,200.

In 1937, Fr. James Keane, OSM, founded here the Perpetual Novena in Honor of Our Sorrowful Mother. At its peak in the late 1930s and 1940s, the novena attracted more than 70,000 persons to 38 novena services every Friday. The service spread to 2,000 other churches and chapels around the world. Because of the influence of the novena and the church's architectural and artistic significance, Pope Pius XII named it a basilica in 1956.

In 1993, the new National Shrine of St. Peregrine was dedicated in one of the nave chapels. St. Peregrine was a fourteenth-century Servite brother who was healed of cancer after praying all night before an image of Christ crucified. He is the patron saint of those living with cancer and other life-threatening diseases.

The basilica and national shrine are open Monday through Saturday, 8:00 a.m.– 4:00 p.m. When the basilica is locked, enter through the adjoining monastery.

SCHEDULE OF MASSES

Sunday: 10:30 a.m.

Monday–Saturday: 8:30 a.m.

DEVOTIONS

Sorrowful Mother Novena: Fridays, 8:00 a.m., 5:00 p.m.

Healing Mass: First Saturday of the month, 11:00 a.m.

Mass for the Sick and Blessing with St. Peregrine Relic: Third Saturday
    of the month, 11:00 a.m.

St. Peregrine Feast Day Mass: First Sunday of May, 2:00 p.m.

Our Lady of Sorrows Feast Day Mass: Third Sunday of September, 10:30 a.m.

St. Peregrine Holy Hour: First Sunday of November, 2:00 p.m.

Special liturgies, novena services, and other devotions may be arranged for
    pilgrimage groups.

FACILITIES

Gift Shop

Museum

Hospitality Room

Cloister Garden

St. Frances X. Cabrini Chapel and National Shrine

ARCHDIOCESE OF CHICAGO • C/O COLUMBUS HOSPITAL
2520 N. LAKEVIEW AVENUE • CHICAGO, IL 60614 • (773) 338-7338

HISTORY OF THE SHRINE

 The shrine is located in Columbus Hospital on the shores of Lake Michigan. The hospital continues its mission of health care in the spirit of its foundress, St. Frances Xavier Cabrini. At the request of Archbishop Quigley of Chicago, Reverend Mother Frances X. Cabrini of the Missionary Sisters of the Sacred Heart established Columbus Hospital on February 25, 1905. It was expanded first in 1920 and, subsequently, in 1950 and 1958.

The south wing of the hospital, adjacent to the St. Frances X. Cabrini Chapel, contains rooms in which our first American citizen saint lived while in Chicago. It is there that she died on December 22, 1917. Mother Cabrini was canonized in 1946. The shrine has been restored to its original simplicity for the benefit of thousands of visitors who come seeking peace, comfort, and consolation.

The major celebrations of the year are the Feast of St. Frances X. Cabrini on November 13 and the Feast of the Sacred Heart in June.

SCHEDULE OF MASSES

Sunday Vigil: 4:00 p.m.
Sunday: 10:00 a.m.
Monday–Friday: 11:30 a.m., 3:45 p.m.

Saturday: 8:00 a.m.
Holy Days of Obligation: 10:00 a.m.
Confessions: Upon request

DEVOTIONS

Novena: Sunday, after 10:00 a.m. Mass
Services for employees and patients are held in the hospital chapel

FACILITIES

Religious Bookstore and Gift Shop
Access to Pastoral Care Staff of the Hospital

TOURS

Upon request

National Shrine of St. Therese

DIOCESE OF JOLIET
8501 BAILEY ROAD • DARIEN, IL 60561-8417 • (630) 969-3311 • FAX (630) 969-5536
INTERNET: HTTP://WWW.CARMELNET.ORG

HISTORY OF THE SHRINE

 The shrine, situated on fifty acres of land at the intersection of Interstate 55 and Cass Avenue, is staffed by the Carmelites, who have been in Darien since 1959. This new shrine was constructed in 1987 to replace the one at St. Clara's Church in Chicago that burned down in 1976.

The St. Therese Shrine consists of a chapel and museum. The shrine chapel contains a stained- and faceted-glass wall depicting the traditions of Carmel. A 12′ x 27′ wood sculpture depicts the events in the hidden life of St. Therese—to lead many to God through her "Shower of Roses" and her "Little Way." The sculpture honors people of all races and cultures who, like Therese, go to God with confidence and love, often touching many lives in hidden but beautiful ways. At the base of the sculpture, an ornate reliquary contains the relics of St. Therese.

The St. Therese museum has not only copies of photos of the Carmelite saint but an original oil painting done by her sister Celine. On display as well are a map of North America drawn by Therese at age twelve, toys, a prayer book from her childhood, and even the chair in which she wrote her autobiography. This is said to be the best collection of relics and memorabilia outside of Therese's native France.

The property also includes a retreat house and retirement complex. Group tours can be arranged by calling the director of the shrine. The shrine is open daily 10:00 a.m.–4:00 p.m. and is closed holidays.

SCHEDULE OF MASSES
Monday–Friday: 11:30 a.m.

DEVOTIONS
Feast of Our Lady of Mt. Carmel: July 16
Feast of St. Therese: October 1

FACILITIES
Religious Bookstore
Religious Gift Shop
Museum
Retreat House

St. Maximilian Kolbe Shrine

ARCHDIOCESE OF CHICAGO
1600 W. PARK AVENUE • LIBERTYVILLE, IL 60048-2593 • (847) 367-7800

HISTORY OF THE SHRINE

This shrine of the Conventual Franciscan Friars reflects the spirit of the work that St. Maximilian Kolbe began at Niepokalonow (Marytown) in Poland. St. Maximilian died in 1941 after he offered his life for a fellow prisoner in the infamous Auschwitz concentration camp. Kolbe was canonized in 1982 as a "Martyr of Charity." Pope John Paul II called him "the prophet of the civilization of love."

The purpose of the shrine is to spread St. Maximilian's work of personal consecration to Mary Immaculate. The generic name of "Marytown" signifies the centrality of Mary in the activities and ministry at the shrine.

The life of this heroic Franciscan is captured on several mosaics depicting various moments of grace in St. Maximilian's life. The newly renovated Kolbe Shrine Chapel is situated within Marytown's exquisite eucharistic sanctuary. The church, a replica of St. Paul's outside-the-wall in Rome, was built to commemorate the twenty-eighth International Eucharistic Congress held in Chicago in 1926. Perpetual Adoration of the Blessed Sacrament is maintained in this beautiful church; it is open 24 hours, daily.

Marytown is ideal for days of recollection, group pilgrimages, and private retreats. A yearlong lay volunteer program is available for young men interested in personal discernment and spiritual growth. The National Center of the Militia Immaculata (MI) movement, founded by St. Maximilian Kolbe in 1917, is located at Marytown.

SCHEDULE OF MASSES
Monday–Saturday: noon

DEVOTIONS
Rosary and Benediction: Daily: 7:00 p.m.
Public Adoration of the Blessed Sacrament: Daily, 24 hours
Liturgy of the Hours: Daily, 7:00 a.m., 11:45 a.m., 5:00 p.m., 7:00 p.m.
First Friday and Saturday devotions
Scripture Study: Weekly
MI Focus Group: Weekly
Secular Franciscan Fraternity: Monthly
Novenas: Weekly and Monthly

FACILITIES

Religious Bookstore and Gift Shop
Conference and Meeting Facilities
Overnight Accommodations

National Shrine of Mary Immaculate Queen of the Universe

DIOCESE OF JOLIET
1025 E. MADISON • LOMBARD, IL 60148 • (630) 627-4526

HISTORY OF THE SHRINE

Devotion to Our Lady as Immaculate Queen of the Universe originated in Ireland. An Irish nun from Donegal spoke of the title and distributed prayers and pictures of this image around the world. Shrines in honor of Mary Immaculate Queen of the Universe were established and churches, schools, and religious houses were given the title. This devotion spread to the United States.

Most Rev. Romeo Blanchette, bishop of Joliet, gave permission to establish this shrine. In his letter of approval he stated, "The Church has exalted this holy woman above all creatures and has proposed her as a model for men and women, young and old. Her humility, her purity, and her obedience should be models for all of us."

On May 31, 1974, the Feast of the Visitation, Mary Immaculate Queen was solemnly welcomed and enthroned in the parish of St. Pius X in Lombard, Ill. Since then countless homes, schools, and churches have enthroned her in the United States.

SCHEDULE OF MASSES
Sunday Vigil: 5:00 p.m.
Sunday: 7:30 a.m., 9:00 a.m., 10:30 a.m., noon
Holy Day of Obligation Vigil: 5:00 p.m.
Holy Day of Obligation: 6:30 a.m., 8:30 a.m., 7:00 p.m.

DEVOTIONS
Rosary and Benediction: Wednesday, 8:00 p.m.

National Shrine of St. Anne

DIOCESE OF JOLIET

230 N. SIXTH STREET • ST. ANNE, IL 60964 • (815) 427-8265

HISTORY OF THE SHRINE

St. Anne, Ill., is a village of about 1,500 residents. It is situated about 10 miles east of Kankakee and 60 miles southwest of Chicago.

The Church of St. Anne was founded in 1852 and built in 1872. The first novena to honor St. Anne was celebrated in St. Anne, Ill., in 1884.

This shrine was established to provide parishioners with a counterpart to the shrine at Beaupre, Canada, and to provide the French-Canadian settlers with the opportunity to make their accustomed pilgrimages to honor St. Anne, especially on her feast day, July 26.

On pilgrimage days and during the novena, pilgrims are given the opportunity to venerate the relics of St. Anne.

Seeing the shrine for the first time, one is impressed by the rows of votive candles before the figure of St. Anne and an ancient wooden wheelchair, crutches, and canes alongside the statue. These are all signs of those who have offered prayers for restored health or for the obtaining of favors. Each year, beginning on July 18 and ending on July 26, a novena to St. Anne is celebrated with Masses, processions, and the veneration of the relics of St. Anne.

SCHEDULE OF MASSES
Sunday Vigil: 4:30 p.m.
Sunday: 9:00 a.m.
Holy Day of Obligation Vigil: 8:00 a.m. (Winter); 7:00 p.m. (Summer)
Holy Day of Obligation: 4:30 p.m. (Winter); 5:15 p.m. (Summer)

DEVOTIONS
Novena to St. Anne: July 18–26

FACILITIES
Religious Gift Shop

The Grotto of the Redemption

DIOCESE OF SIOUX CITY
P.O. BOX 376 • WEST BEND, IA 50597 • (515) 887-2371

HISTORY OF THE SHRINE

 The Grotto of the Redemption at West Bend, Iowa, is the largest grotto in the world. It is sometimes considered "the eighth wonder of the world." The grotto represents the largest collection of minerals and petrification concentrated in any one spot in the world. Fr. Paul Dobberstein started construction on the grotto in 1912. For forty-two years, he labored setting ornamental rocks and gems into concrete. By his death in 1954, he had created the incredible "Grotto of the Redemption," covering one city block. Since his death, Fr. Louis Greving, who had worked with Fr. Dobberstein for eight years, has been continuing construction on the grotto. Fr. Greving retired in 1996. Deacon Gerlad Streit is now director of the grotto.

The grotto is a composite of nine separate grottoes, each portraying a scene in the life of Christ in his work of redeeming the world. More than 100,000 people visit the grotto annually. The grotto is open to visitors year-round. There are hourly tours through the grotto from June 1 to October 15. After every hourly tour, a geological lecture is given in the rock display studio; this lecture identifies the materials used in the grotto and features an ultraviolet light display. The grotto is flooded with spotlights for evening viewing. There is no fee for viewing the grotto, however a $3.00 donation per adult is suggested.

Adjacent to the grotto is St. Peter and Paul's Church. The Christmas chapel in the church is Fr. Dobberstein's finest work. It contains a Brazilian amethyst that weighs more than three hundred pounds.

SCHEDULE OF MASSES
Sunday Vigil: 5:00 p.m.
Sunday: (Daylight time) 9:00 a.m., (Standard time) 9:30 a.m.

FACILITIES
Restaurant (reservations requested for large groups)
Gift Store
Museum
Picnic Area
Overnight Campground with electrical hookups. (Donations accepted.)

Shrine of St. Philippine Duchesne

ARCHDIOCESE OF KANSAS CITY IN KANSAS
SACRED HEART CHURCH • MOUND CITY, KS 66056 • (913) 795-2724

HISTORY OF THE SHRINE

 St. Philippine Duchesne cared for the needs of the Potawatomi Indians at St. Mary's Indian Mission, twelve miles northwest of the shrine. In 1941, the late Bishop Paul C. Schulte of the Diocese of Leavenworth, Kan. (now the Archdiocese of Kansas City, Kan.) collected funds from the parishes and people of the diocese to build a stone church and rectory complete with furnishings. The church was dedicated as a memorial shrine to St. Philippine Duchesne on September 7, 1942.

The church is 100 feet long and 40 feet wide, built of stone from St. Mary's Indian Mission. The 125-acre St. Philippine Memorial Park was purchased and developed through the efforts of Fr. Robert Pool, once pastor here, and Robert White, a Catholic layman from Overland Park, Kans. Pilgrimages have been held at both places throughout the years. The memorial park was dedicated by Archbishop Ignatius Strecker on July 3, 1988, the date of St. Philippine's canonization by Pope John Paul II.

The Shrine of St. Philippine Duchesne celebrated its Golden Jubilee of the parish in 1992.

SCHEDULE OF MASSES
Saturday: 7:00 p.m.
Weekdays: 8:00 a.m.
Holy Day of Obligation: 7:00 p.m.
Confessions: Anytime

DEVOTIONS
Daily: Novena Prayers to St. Philippine Duchesne
First Friday Devotions
First Saturday Devotions
Pilgrimage tours of the shrine in Mound City and the memorial park with Mass, upon request. Call (913) 755-2652.

Shrine of St. Anne

ARCHDIOCESE OF DETROIT
1000 ST. ANNE STREET • DETROIT, MI 48216 • (313) 496-1701

HISTORY OF THE SHRINE

St. Anne's is the oldest parish in Detroit, dating back to the founding of the city in 1701. Fr. Gabriel Richard (1767–1832), the famous pastor, is buried in the church. The shrine has been approved by Rome as one of the shrines of St. Anne. Today, the parish has a predominantly Hispanic congregation.

A novena is celebrated July 16–26. A former pastor, Fr. Luke Renaud, encouraged this devotion, which became an important event in Catholic life. A festival is held around the time of the novena. The Feast of Guadalupe is observed on December 12.

SCHEDULE OF MASSES

Sunday Vigil: 5:00 p.m.
Sunday: 8:30 a.m., 10:00 a.m. (Spanish), noon
Holy Day of Obligation Vigil: 5:00 p.m.
Holy Day of Obligation: 8:30 a.m., noon, 5:15 p.m., 7:00 p.m. (Spanish)
Confessions: Saturday: 4:00–5:00 p.m., 7:00–8:00 p.m.

DEVOTIONS

Novenas: Weekly
Bible Class: Weekly (Spanish)

FACILITIES

Gift Shop

LANGUAGES

English and Spanish

The Cross in the Woods

DIOCESE OF GAYLORD
7078 M-68 • INDIAN RIVER, MI 49749 • (616) 238-8973

HISTORY OF THE SHRINE

Blessed Kateri Tekakwitha, often called the "Lily of the Mohawks," was the inspiration for this shrine in Indian River. The first pastor, Msgr. Charles D. Brophy, had a devotion to Blessed Kateri. Born in 1656, the Indian maiden converted to the Catholic faith at the age of eighteen and suffered much because of her faith. Her practice of erecting crosses in the woods around the village, as reminders of her Lord and as places to pray, gave the first pastor the idea of erecting the huge cross at the shrine.

The centerpiece of the shrine, the cross, is made from a 55-foot redwood tree. Renowned sculptor Marshall Fredericks created a bronze seven-ton image of the crucified Christ, which was raised into place in 1959. The shrine has been inspiring visitors since it establishment in 1946.

The complex includes a large outdoor sanctuary seating 650, where the eucharist is offered during the summer months. A new church was erected in 1997. Its front wall of glass makes visiting and praying before the cross possible year-round.

During a visit to the shrine, people may make the Stations of the Cross in a secluded area of the grounds. Shrines honoring the Blessed Mother; St. Peregrine, the patron of cancer patients; Blessed Kateri; and St. Francis of Assisi are also available for prayer.

Of special interest to visitors is a unique collection of 525 dolls dressed in the habits of nuns who served the Church in the United States. A gift store offers visitors a wide variety of religious articles and spiritual reading material.

The peaceful quiet strength that Blessed Kateri Tekakwitha drew from God and nature seems to permeate the shrine, beckoning people of all Christian faiths to prayer and reflection on the Lord's love for us. The shrine is staffed by Franciscans of the Sacred Heart Province of St. Louis, Province. It is located on M-68, two minutes off Hwy I-75, exit 310.

In 1995, AAA members voted the shrine as the "Most Beautiful Place of Worship in Michigan."

SCHEDULE OF MASSES
Last Weekend in June through Labor Day
Sunday Vigil: 4:30 p.m., 6:00 p.m.
Sunday: 8:30 a.m., 10:30 a.m.
Daily: 8:30 a.m., noon
Confessions: Upon request

FACILITIES
Outdoor Sanctuary
Gift Shop

St. Mary's of Mount Carmel Shrine

DIOCESE OF GAYLORD
260 ST. MARY'S PARKWAY • MANISTEE, MI 49660 • (616) 723-3345

HISTORY OF THE SHRINE

St. Mary's was the first Catholic parish in Manistee and was formed in 1862. It became the mother church for the area and for other parishes that followed. St. Mary's was known as the "French Church."

The present church, constructed as a shrine in 1962, is the third St. Mary's in Manistee. The flowing roof design and huge beams were constructed to follow the form of the sand dunes of Lake Michigan, which is within sight. The white marble came from Georgia, the red granite from Wisconsin, and the gray granite altar from South Dakota. The marble in the five wall murals came from Tennessee; the tile mural came from and was made in Canada. The outdoor Stations of the Cross came from the old church. Twenty Madonna Shrine wood carvings from Italy represent various titles of Mary.

The central focus of the shrine is a 10-foot statue of Our Lady of Mt. Carmel carved in Italy by Vincenzo Demetz, from a block of linden wood from Yugoslavia. The statue, an original, weighs 480 pounds and took more than two years to complete.

The rosary is recited before weekend services. The months of May and October are special times to visit the shrine. The Feast of Our Lady of Mt. Carmel is on July 16.

SCHEDULE OF MASSES
Sunday Vigil: 5:00 p.m.
Sunday: 8:30 a.m., 11:00 a.m.
Confessions: 30 minutes before Mass

St. Mary Shrine

DIOCESE OF GAYLORD
201 M-72 • MIO, MI 48647 • (517) 826-5509

HISTORY OF THE SHRINE

The shrine-grotto at Mio, Mich., is a composite of shrines, a mountainous structure of stone honeycombed with grottos and niches.

The name, "Our Lady of the Woods," reflects the thousands of acres of God's beautiful and majestic timberlands visible from the shrine. These regions, once home to the lumberjack, are now meccas to hunters, fishermen, and tourists.

Viewed from the front, the shrine is a sloping triangle of stone. It slowly rises from the ground on two sides, ending in a peak, pointing out that all humankind's destiny is heavenwards, that the natural and temporal should be sublimated into the spiritual and eternal. One can also visualize two arms forming from the peak of this monument as if to embrace the entire state of Michigan, the country, and the world.

The shrine-grotto is replete with symbolism, including an outdoor chapel and sanctuary. Various statues are placed throughout the grotto, including the Infant of Prague, the Resurrection, St. Hubert, and St. Anne de Beaupre. The major Marian shrines are represented by Our Lady of Lourdes, Our Lady of Fatima, Our Lady of La Salette, Our Lady of Czestochowa, the Assumption, and Our Lady of Guadalupe. Everything possible has been done to make the Mother of Christ appear at home in Michigan.

SCHEDULE OF MASSES
Sunday Vigil: 5:00 p.m.
Sunday: 8:00 a.m., 10:00 a.m.

FACILITIES
Gift Shop, open weekends Memorial Day–Labor Day

Assumption of Our Lady Chapel

DIOCESE OF ST. CLOUD
CHAPEL STREET • COLD SPRING, MN 56320 • (612) 685-3280

HISTORY OF THE SHRINE

This chapel is a memorial to the divine help received during the grasshopper plague more than a century ago. It was built through the inspiration of Bishop Peter W. Bartholome, the fifth bishop of St. Cloud, and was solemnly dedicated on October 7, 1952, the Feast of the Most Holy Rosary.

The construction of this chapel was zealously supervised by Fr. Victor Ronellenfitsch, OSB, the pastor of St. Boniface Church, Cold Spring; the architect was his assistant, Fr. Athanase Fuchs, OSB. The Cold Spring Granite Company and its workers were the chief donors of the material and labor.

The 16' x 26' chapel is built of rough pink-gray granite with a reddish shingled roof topped by a belfry and a stainless-steel cross. The imported stained-glass windows depict scenes in the life of the Blessed Mother. On the wall behind the altar is a statue of the Blessed Mother.

In honor of the 1950 definition of the Assumption of the Blessed Mother by Pope Pius XII, the chapel was renamed Assumption Chapel. Over the chapel entrance is a tympanum with a relief of the Blessed Mother and the words, *Asumpta est Maria*. At her feet, two grasshoppers kneel in humble submission.

An earlier chapel, called Grasshopper Chapel, was built in 1877, commemorating the Blessed Virgin Mary's intercession in sparing the farmers and people of Central Minnesota during the grasshopper plague. In 1877, the pastors and parishioners of several parishes in Central Minnesota vowed to honor Mary with special devotions at the site each year. This has been done faithfully each year since 1877 on the Feast of the Assumption.

SCHEDULE OF MASSES

August 15, Feast of the Assumption (Mass is celebrated by the bishop.)

National Shrine of St. Odilia

DIOCESE OF ST. CLOUD

CROSIER FATHERS AND BROTHERS • BOX 500, ONAMIA, MN 56359-0500 • (320) 532-3103

HISTORY OF THE SHRINE

The Shrine of St. Odilia was established in 1952 when a major relic of the saint was brought to Onamia, Minn. In 1287, St. Odilia appeared to John Novelan, a lay brother of the Crosier Order in Paris, and told him she had been appointed by God to be the patron saint and the protectress of the Order of the Holy Cross. She informed him that her relics were located in an orchard in Cologne and begged him to get permission to unearth them.

St. Odilia had instructed Brother John that her relics were to be taken to the mother-house of the order at Huy, Belgium. Both at Cologne and on the way to Huy, various cures of physical infirmities took place.

During the French Revolution, the monastery at Huy was destroyed, and, although the relics were saved, they were lost to the order. In 1949, St. Odilia came back home. Her relics were returned to the order, and a large portion of one of her bones was brought to Onamia, and now rests in her shrine here, where it is encased in a marble reliquary.

St. Odilia has promised to shower a stream of graces upon the Crosier Fathers and upon all those who invoke her aid in their hour of need. For centuries it has been the practice of the Crosier Order to bless water in honor of St. Odilia by dipping her relic in it and asking God to give it power against all diseases and bodily infirmities. Through her intercession, many are cured, especially from ailments of the eyes.

SCHEDULE OF MASSES
Daily

DEVOTIONS
The St. Odilia Novena begins on the 5th and 17th of each month. The National Novena to St. Odilia is held July 10–18. Intentions for this novena can be mailed to the shrine and visitors can participate in the novena. St. Odilia devotional items may be obtained by writing to the shrine.

TOURS
On request

National Shrine of Our Lady of the Miraculous Medal

ARCHDIOCESE OF ST. LOUIS • ST. MARY'S OF THE BARRENS
1811 W. ST. JOSEPH STREET • PERRYVILLE, MO 63775-1598 • (573) 547-8344
1-800-264-MARY • INTERNET: HTTP://WWW.AMM.ORG/VISIT.HTM • E-MAIL: VISIT@AMM.ORG

HISTORY OF THE SHRINE

The National Shrine of Our Lady of the Miraculous Medal is located in St. Mary's of the Barrens Historic District, established in 1818. The church where the shrine is located was begun in 1827 and was consecrated in 1837. The shrine chapel was built in 1929–30 for the one hundredth anniversary of the apparition of Mary to St. Catherine Labouré at Paris in 1830. For more than a century, the shrine site was the seminary for the priests and brothers of the Congregation of the Mission (Vincentians). St. Mary's of the Barrens is the first establishment of the Vincentians in the western hemisphere.

The main religious celebrations are the May procession held on the first Sunday in May, the Rose Rosary Novena held October 7–15, and the Christmas Novena, held December 16–24. The average attendance at the May procession is about 1,000. Approximately 5,000 pilgrims register at the shrine annually. About 10,000 votive lights burn day and night in the shrine as a sign of the prayers and intentions offered through the Association of the Miraculous Medal.

SCHEDULE OF MASSES
Sunday: 11:00 a.m.
Daily: 8:00 a.m.
Confessions: Monday, 7:00 p.m. and by arrangement

DEVOTIONS
Novenas: Monday, 7:15 p.m. (Miraculous Medal Novena and Mass)

FACILITIES:
Museums
Gift Shop: Monday–Friday, 9:00 a.m.–noon, 1:00–4:30 p.m.; Saturday, 1:00–4:30 p.m.; Sunday, noon–4:30 p.m. Closed holy days, holidays, January and February.

TOURS

Guided Tours: Saturday–Sunday, 1:00 p.m., 3:00 p.m.; March–December: Monday–Friday, 10:00 a.m., 1:00 p.m.; weekday tours during January and February are available by arrangement. No tours on holy days and holidays.

Guided group tours by appointment are welcome. Arrangements can be made for a catered meal for groups of 15 or more. Accessible to people with disabilities.

Shrine of St. Philippine Duchesne

ARCHDIOCESE OF ST. LOUIS
619 N. SECOND STREET • ST. CHARLES, MO 63301 • (314) 946-6127

HISTORY OF THE SHRINE

This shrine, on the campus of the Academy of the Sacred Heart, was built in 1952 in honor of St. Philippine Duchesne. A marble sarcophagus, holding the saintly remains of Philippine Duchesne, is in an alcove facing the altar in the shrine.

Rose Philippine Duchesne, a French Religious of the Sacred Heart, started the first free school west of the Mississippi River in a log cabin in 1818. The first permanent building was constructed in 1835.

As visitors walk through the parlors of this building, a guide tells them how Philippine Duchesne left her native France and settled in the wilderness that was St. Charles. They learn that Philippine Duchesne started other schools in Louisiana and St. Louis and how this humble beginning in the New World has blossomed into a network of nineteen Sacred Heart schools in the United States. Pilgrims may also see the room in which this saint died in 1852. The shrine is open daily for prayer and visits. A schedule of guided tours and group tour information is available.

DEVOTIONS

The Feast of St. Philippine Duchesne: November 18
Christmas Eve Mass
First Communion

FACILITIES

Gift Shop
Museum

Shrine of Our Lady of Levocha

DIOCESE OF CLEVELAND
1160 BROADWAY • BEDFORD, OH 44146 • (216) 232-4755

HISTORY OF THE SHRINE

This is an outdoor shrine located on the property of the motherhouse of the Vincentian Sisters of Charity of the Diocese of Cleveland. The shrine was established in 1930. It is the only National Shrine of Our Lady of Levocha in America. The statue of Our Lady of Levocha was carved from the wood of an apple tree under the direction of Bishop John Vojtassak of Slovakia and was touched to the original statue of Our Lady before being shipped to the United States.

Although the early pilgrims were from Slovak backgrounds, people of all nationalities have come to honor Our Lady as individuals, groups, and on special pilgrimage days. They come to unburden their hearts and to seek consolation and aid for themselves and for their loved ones.

Because there is no resident priest to offer daily Mass, pilgrims come to make private visits to Our Lady from the first Sunday of May until the official closing of the shrine on the first Sunday of October.

DEVOTIONS

Annual (traditional) Pilgrimage Day: July 2
Feasts of Saints Joachim and Ann: July 26 (this special pilgrimage day draws more than 500 people)

LANGUAGES

Services are conducted in English and Slovak

Sorrowful Mother Shrine

DIOCESE OF TOLEDO
4106 STATE ROUTE #269 • BELLEVUE, OH 44811• (419) 483-3435

HISTORY OF THE SHRINE

 The shrine was founded in 1850 on four acres. It now encompasses 140 acres, of which seventy are virgin forest, accommodating the Stations of the Cross, ten grottoes, various statues, and more than a mile of paved paths. The Stations were added during World War I, the Lourdes and Sepulchre grottoes in the 1930s, and later the grottoes to Our Lady of Guadalupe and Assumption, Fatima, and Our Lady of Czestochowa. The cafeteria, religious goods store, and 1,000 seat outdoor pavilion were added in 1960.

On Sundays and holy days, clergy lead devout processions, making stops at each sacred grotto along the Way of the Cross. Frequent processions, outdoor Masses, and the old shrine chapel provide devotional experiences that keep pilgrims returning.

The ethnic celebrations are a big attraction, but many pilgrims come seeking solace in the peaceful wooded area.

Sponsored by Missionaries of the Precious Blood.

SCHEDULE OF MASSES
Sunday Vigil: 4:30 p.m.
Sunday: 9:00 a.m., 11:00 a.m.
Daily: 11:00 a.m., 4:30 p.m.
Holy Day of Obligation Vigil: 4:30 p.m.
Holy Day of Obligation: 9:00 a.m., 11:00 a.m.
Confessions: Daily, 4:00 p.m.; Sunday, 8:30 a.m., 9:30 a.m., 10:30 a.m.

DEVOTIONS
Mass and Devotion schedules are adapted for pilgrimage groups.
Processions, Rosary, Benediction: Sunday
Novenas: Monthly
Days of Recollection: Weekly

FACILITIES
Religious Bookstore
Gift Shop
Cafeteria

LANGUAGES
English, Italian, Chaldean, Slovak, Spanish, Slovenian, Tagalog, and Polish

The Shrine will be celebrating its 150th anniversary during the Jubilee Year 2000.

The Shrine and Church of Mariapoch

BYZANTINE CATHOLIC EPARCHY OF PARMA

17486 MUMFORD ROAD • BURTON, OH 44021 • (216) 834-8807 • (216) 834-4078

HISTORY OF THE SHRINE

 The shrine is located in southern Geauga County, one mile north of Route 422 on Mumford Road. This shrine was dedicated and blessed by the Byzantine Catholic bishop, Most. Rev. Nicholas Elko, in 1956. The original Shrine of Mariapoch is in northeastern Hungary and began more than 300 years ago, in 1696. A Byzantine icon of the Mother of God holding the Christ child began weeping tears from Mary's eyes for eighteen days, until December 8, while miracles of faith, conversion, and healing were reported and later confirmed by an ecclesial commission that studied the reports. Increasing numbers of pilgrims journeyed to Poch from neighboring villages and more distant regions, bringing people from varying religious and ethnic backgrounds.

The Shrine of Mariapoch was and is held in high esteem by the people of Hungary, where it is located today in the jurisdiction of the Byzantine Catholic Bishop Keresztes Szilard, eparch of Hajdudorog, Hungary. Later, immigrants came to the United States with cherished memories of the original shrine and their experiences. An anonymous donor offered fifty acres to establish a similar Shrine of Our Lady of Mariapoch in the Burton, Ohio area. History records that two miraculous icons of Our Lady of Mariapoch exist. The original one is now in St. Stephen's Basilica in Vienna, Austria; a second icon, ordered in the early eighteenth century by Emperor Leopold, also wept on several occasions around 1905. The Shrine of Mariapoch in Burton, Ohio holds two mosaic replicas of these icons within the Shrine Altar sanctuary for pilgrims to pray before.

The Byzantine Catholic Eparchy first administered the Mariapoch Shrine in 1969 by the late Bishop Emil J. Mihalik, DD, later by Most Rev. Andrew Pataki, DD, and now by Most Rev. Basil Schott, DD, OFM, who became bishop of the Parma Eparchy in 1996. The Parma Eparchy celebrates its Annual Eparchial Pilgrimage to the Shrine of Mariapoch the second Sunday of August, with concluding services August 15, Feast of the Dormition of the Mother of God.

SCHEDULE OF MASSES

Saturday: 11:00 a.m. Divine Liturgy
Sunday: 11:00 a.m. Divine Liturgy,
Reconciliation: Sunday, 10:15–10:45 a.m., 2:45–3:15 p.m.

DEVOTIONS

Marian Devotions: Sunday, 3:30 p.m. Akathist Service or Paraklis Service
Public Anointing of the Sick: First Sunday, May–October, following 3:30 p.m. Service

FACILITIES

Shrine Church (open year round)
Outdoor Shrine Altar (open May–first Sunday in October)
Gift and Book Shop
Cafeteria
Mosaic Triptych Icon of Mary's Appearance over Constantinople
Icon Displays
Sheltered Picnic Area
Guest House for small groups

LANGUAGES

English, Hungarian, and Ruthenian

Basilica and Shrine of Our Lady of Consolation

DIOCESE OF TOLEDO
315 CLAY STREET, CAREY • OH 43316 • (419) 396-7107 • (419) 396-3355

HISTORY OF THE SHRINE

Since 1875, countless numbers of pilgrims have journeyed to the Basilica and Shrine of Our Lady of Consolation to express their devotion to Mary, Consoler of the Afflicted. Devotion to this image of Mary was first expressed by St. Ignatius of Antioch in the second century. In the seventeenth century, when an outbreak of bubonic plague devastated the population, the people of the Grand Duchy of Luxembourg began praying to Mary, and a small chapel was built on the outskirts of town to enshrine her image. In 1652, Pope Innocent X established a confraternity at the little shrine.

The devotion flourished for two hundred years and then spread to North America, where the first shrine was established by Fr. Joseph P. Gloden at the mission of Carey, Ohio. The people of Carey had their wood frame Mission Church of St. Edward rededicated under the title of Our Lady of Consolation to house this image. Patronal Feast Day is celebrated May 25 each year. The 125th Anniversary Celebrations will coincide with the Jubilee in the year 2000. A replica of the original image was brought to nearby Frenchtown, and from there a solemn procession took it to the little church at Carey.

On April 28, 1878, Pope Leo XIII established a confraternity at Carey, thus firmly establishing the devotion of Our Lady of Consolation in this country. In 1925, a new and larger church was dedicated, and in 1971 Pope Paul VI designated it a minor basilica.

The shrine is a noted location for the healing of body, mind, and spirit through the intercession of Our Lady of Consolation.

The shrine is open for prayer twenty-four hours a day. Pilgrimage groups visit the shrine from May through October, when six different Catholic rites are celebrated; groups of many nationalities join in the festivities during the month of August.

SCHEDULE OF MASSES

Sunday Vigil: 5:30 p.m.
Sunday: Easter–November 1, 8:00 a.m., 10:00 a.m., noon; November 1–Easter,
     9:00 a.m., 11:00 a.m.
Weekdays: 7:00 a.m., 11:00 a.m.
Saturday: 7:00 a.m., 11:00 a.m.

DEVOTIONS

Benediction of the Blessed Sacrament, Healing Service: Sunday, 2:30 p.m. (including
     Marian devotions)
Rosary Procession: May–October, every Sunday with statues carried in procession
Our Lady of Consolation Feast Day: May 25
Candlelight Procession and Mass: August 14

FACILITIES

Renewal Center (for retreats and overnight pilgrimages)
Overnight Accommodations
Cafeteria
Gift Shop
Thirty-five acre Outdoor Shrine Park
Ample Car and Bus Parking

National Friary and Shrine of St. Anthony

ARCHDIOCESE OF CINCINNATI
FRANCISCAN FRIARS • 5000 COLERAIN AVENUE • CINCINNATI, OH 45223 • (513) 541-2146

HISTORY OF THE SHRINE

 Mr. and Mrs. A. Joseph Nurre, devout members of St. Francis Seraph Parish, bought a country estate high above Cincinnati for the local Franciscan Friars and promised to build a monastery, a home for infirm friars, and a chapel to serve as a Franciscan novitiate. The cornerstone was laid and blessed by Fr. Jerome, a former provincial superior, in 1888. In October, the first friars moved into the original estate house and on Thanksgiving Day, 1889, Archbishop Henry Elder of Cincinnati consecrated the chapel. The first investitures at Mt. Airy, the familiar name for the friary and shrine, took place on the Feast of the Assumption in 1890.

The chapel was dedicated to St. Anthony; however, it was never intended to be a shrine. Gradually, people began to make private pilgrimages to the chapel, and, as the number of visitors increased, the chapel became known as St. Anthony's Shrine. Furnishings for the shrine came from France, Belgium, Bavaria, Holland, and Austria. Originally the shrine contained eight side altars. Above the high altar were two large paintings portraying scenes from the life of St. Anthony; however, these paintings were covered over when the shrine was redecorated in 1978.

In January 1928, a small group of friends met at the friary at the invitation of Fr. Stephen Hoffmann, OFM, in order to establish a society to further devotion to St. Anthony and to promote the upkeep of the shrine. They built a beautiful shelter-house in which to serve refreshments to visitors, which has now been replaced by the hall. The society is also responsible for welcoming and accommodating visitors and for organizing the annual festival in September.

SCHEDULE OF MASSES
Sunday: 10:00 a.m.
Weekdays: 7:30 a.m.
Saturday: 8:15 a.m.
Holy Days: 7:30 a.m.
Christmas and New Year's Day: 10:00 a.m.
Novena Mass: Tuesday, 7:00 p.m.
Confessions: Tuesday, 3:00–5:00 p.m.

DEVOTIONS

Novena to St. Anthony: Tuesday, 2:30 p.m.
Feast of St. Anthony: June 13 (blessing of bread)
Solemn Novena of Nine Tuesdays before the Feast of St. Anthony
Petitions to St. Anthony can be mailed into the shrine.
Lighting of Vigil Candles can be requested through the mail.

St. Paul Shrine

DIOCESE OF CLEVELAND
CONVERSION OF ST. PAUL CHURCH • E. 40TH STREET AND EUCLID AVENUE
CLEVELAND, OH 44103 • (216) 431-8854

HISTORY OF THE SHRINE

Established in 1931 as the Church of the Conversion of St. Paul and Shrine of the Blessed Sacrament, the church came to be known simply as St. Paul Shrine. The Monastery of the Poor Clares of Perpetual Adoration is attached to the shrine. Nuns maintain prayerful vigil before the Blessed Sacrament exposed throughout the day. Capuchin Franciscans minister to the sisters, the small parish community, and visitors.

SCHEDULE OF MASSES

Sunday: 11:30 a.m.
Daily: noon
Holy Day of Obligation: noon
Confessions: Monday–Saturday, 11:30 a.m.

DEVOTIONS

Novenas: Monday–Friday following noon Mass
Perpetual Adoration of the Blessed Sacrament: Daily, 9:00 a.m.–1:00 p.m.

FACILITIES

Daily meal for the needy

National Shrine of Our Lady of Lourdes

DIOCESE OF CLEVELAND
21281 CHARDON ROAD • EUCLID, OH 44117-1591 • (216) 481-8232

HISTORY OF THE SHRINE

 The shrine and grotto of Our Lady of Lourdes at Euclid, Ohio, is a copy of the original shrine in Lourdes, France. In 1922, while visiting the world-famous shrine at Lourdes, Mother Mary of St. John Berchmans McGarvey was inspired to erect a similar grotto on the property of the Good Shepherd Sisters in Euclid. Fr. Pere Ekert, a Dominican priest, gave the sisters a piece of stone hewn of the rock on which the Blessed Mother stood when she appeared to Bernadette. Two pieces of the stone are now imbedded in the grotto, and the other is located in a reliquary in the Gift Shop.

Bishop Joseph Schrembs, DD, blessed and dedicated the grotto on Trinity Sunday, May 30, 1926. On the occasion of a city-wide pilgrimage October 7, 1928, Bishop Schrembs conferred the title of National American Shrine of Our Lady of Lourdes.

Since the erection of the shrine, pilgrims have come to honor Our Lady and to place their petitions before her. Hundreds of favors, spiritual and temporal, have been granted. Today, the Trinitarian Sisters operate the shrine. Their novitiate and provincial house in the United States are also located here.

SCHEDULE OF MASSES

Sunday: 8:00 a.m. (chapel), 9:30 a.m. (grotto, May–October, weather permitting)
Daily: Monday, Wednesday–Friday, 7:00 a.m.; Tuesday, 5:00 p.m.; Saturday, 8:00 a.m.
Holy Day of Obligation: 8:00 a.m.
Holiday: 8:00 a.m.
Confessions: During Novenas only

DEVOTIONS

Rosary: Daily, 12:30 p.m.
Stations of the Cross: Sunday, 3:00 p.m.; with Rosary Procession, Homily, and
    Benediction, 4:00 p.m. (May–October); Blessing of religious articles in chapel
    after Benediction.

NOVENAS

Our Lady of Lourdes Novena: February 3–11
Triduum and Feast of St. Ann: July 24–26
Assumption Novena: August 7–15
Sisters' Christmas Novena for Benefactors: December 16–24

SPECIAL EVENTS

Last Sunday of June: Italian Day Celebration (services, food, music)
First Sunday of October: Rosary Sunday/Fall Festival, Bazaar

FACILITIES

Gift Shop
St. Ann Dining Room

Shrine of the Holy Relics

ARCHDIOCESE OF CINCINNATI
2291 ST. JOHNS ROAD • MARIA STEIN, OH 45860 • (419) 925-4532

HISTORY OF THE SHRINE

The Shrine of the Holy Relics contains a rare collection of holy relics brought from Italy and donated to the Sisters of the Precious Blood in 1875 by a priest from Milwaukee. In 1892, a beautiful new chapel was opened to house the relics. During this time, the Rev. Francis de Sales Brunner, the first Precious Blood priest to come to America, added relics to the collection.

The relics are the remembrances of the saints of God. The remains of the martyrs were venerated in the catacombs of Rome. In the Middle Ages, people made pilgrimages to shrines that housed these sacred remains for the purpose of prayer. At Maria Stein, the sacred tradition of the Church is continued as people come from near and far in the spirit of prayer and hope to honor the memory of those holy men and women of God. The large number of people who visit the shrine indicates the many graces and favors granted by God through the intercession of saints.

The shrine is staffed by the Sisters of the Precious Blood. There is no resident chaplain; please inquire about Mass.

SPECIAL EVENTS
Upon request

FACILITIES
Religious Gift Shop
Shrine of the Holy Relics: Tuesday–Sunday, 9:30 a.m.–4:30 p.m.
Maria Stein Heritage Museum: First Sunday in May–last Sunday in October,
    Tuesday–Sunday, noon–4:00 p.m.
Pilgrim Gift Shop: Tuesday–Sunday, noon–4:30 p.m.

All facilities closed on Mondays.

National Shrine of Our Lady of Lebanon

DIOCESE OF ST. MARON • EPARCHY OF OUR LADY OF LEBANON
2759 NORTH LIPKEY ROAD • NORTH JACKSON, OH 44451 • (330) 538-3351

HISTORY OF THE SHRINE

The National Shrine of Our Lady of Lebanon is a replica of the original shrine in Harissa, Lebanon. This shrine is Maronite Rite Catholic and was established in 1963 to bring together Lebanese, Syrians, and Americans through the intercession of Our Lady of Lebanon. Like the original Shrine in Lebanon, the replica in North Jackson, Ohio, just 10 miles west of Youngstown, has been a place of pilgrimage for people of all nationalities. Pilgrims of the faith, and those without faith, have come to Our Lady of Lebanon Shrine with their special needs and then return home with many great blessings. The shrine project received the approval of Pope John XXIII and Bishop Emmet M. Walsh, of Youngstown.

The main religious celebration of the year is the Feast of the Assumption in August. The three-day festivities attract numerous pilgrims. The Holy Week and Easter celebrations traditional to Maronite Catholics provide a spiritual and cultural experience for all members of the Roman Catholic faith.

SCHEDULE OF MASSES
Sunday Vigil: 5:30 p.m.
Sunday: 10:00 a.m., 5:30 p.m.
Daily: Monday–Wednesday, 7:30 a.m.; Thursday, 5:30 p.m.; Friday, noon
Confessions: Half-hour before each weekend liturgy and by appointment

DEVOTIONS
Rosary: Daily before Mass
Devotion to Our Lady of Lebanon: Wednesday, 7:00 a.m.
First Friday Liturgy in honor of the Sacred Heart of Jesus: 11:00 a.m. Holy Hour, followed by noon Mass
First Saturday Liturgy in honor of the Immaculate Heart of Mary: 8:00 a.m.
Feast of Our Lady of Lebanon: First Sunday in May
Annual Assumption Pilgrimage: August 13–15

NINE-DAY NOVENAS
March: St. Joseph
September: St. Theresa
October: St. Jude (Triduum)
December: Infant Jesus; Triduum to Our Lady of Guadalupe

FACILITIES
Main Chapel, Christ Prince of Peace
Small Tower Chapel
Religious Bookstore
Gift Shop
Banquet Halls
Outdoor Way of the Cross

LANGUAGES
English, Aramaic, and Lebanese

Shrine of Our Lady, Comforter of the Afflicted

DIOCESE OF YOUNGSTOWN
517 S. BELLE VISTA AVENUE • YOUNGSTOWN, OH 44509 • (330) 799-1888

HISTORY OF THE SHRINE

The Shrine of Our Lady, Comforter of the Afflicted was established in Youngstown, Ohio, by Hungarian Franciscans who fled their homeland shortly after World War II. The shrine is a replica of the original shrine in Transylvania, Hungary, which was closed by the Communist regime.

The shrine in Youngstown continues the charism and the spirit of Our Lady, Comforter of the Afflicted, in Transylvania and serves people across the country, especially those of Hungarian origin. The Franciscan Order staffs the shrine.

SCHEDULE OF MASSES

Sunday: 8:00 a.m., 9:30 a.m., noon
Weekday: Monday–Saturday, 7:00 a.m., noon
Holy Day of Obligation: 8:00 a.m., 9:30 a.m., noon, 7:30 p.m.
Confessions: Monday–Saturday, 11:15–11:55 a.m.; Saturday, 6:00–7:00 p.m. and
   by appointment

DEVOTIONS

Novenas: Weekly and annually
Rosary: Weekly
Retreats: For groups, upon request
Holy Hour of Eucharistic Adoration: Weekly
Pilgrimage on Pentecost Sunday: Annually

FACILITIES

Religious Bookstore
Cafeteria
Counseling Center
Gift Shop
Cultural Center

LANGUAGES

English, Hungarian, and German

Mid-America's Fatima Family Shrine

ST. MARY OF MERCY CHURCH • MOTHER OF MERCY CARMEL MONASTERY
DIOCESE OF SIOUX FALLS
BOX 158 • ALEXANDRIA, SD 57311-0158 • (605) 239-4532

HISTORY OF THE SHRINE

 The shrine honoring the Holy Family and the Holy Eucharist was the fulfillment of the dream of Fr. Robert J. Fox, founder of the Fatima Family Apostolate, which is recognized by the Pontifical Council for the Family. In 1987, he built the outdoor shrine for Mass and candlelight processions, using royalties from his many books and articles written over 30 years.

The shrine—with St. Mary of Mercy Church, which also contains sites honoring the King of Divine Mercy, Our Lady of Guadalupe, and Our Lady of Fatima—is home to the international Fatima Family Apostolate dedicated to the sanctification of the family. Its quarterly publication, *Immaculate Heart Messenger*, goes to many countries.

The shrine church holds 300 people and is an extension to the outdoor shrine. Visitors to the outdoor shrine can make the Stations of the Cross, consecrate their families at the outdoor Holy Family Chapel, and pray before the Pro-Life Shrine of Our Lady of Guadalupe and an image of the Angel of the Family, which have special prayers inscribed at their bases.

Mother of Mercy Carmel, the first contemplative Carmelite Monastery in South Dakota, was built near this beautiful shrine in 1997. Mass is offered daily in its chapel; Carmelite sisters sing the Gregorian Chant on Sundays. Their book store features many books, cassettes, and videos about the Fatima Family Apostolate.

The shrine has drawn thousands of visitors each year, the bishops of Leirla-Fatima in Portugal on three occasions, the cardinal prefect of the Pontifical Council of the Family, and the archbishop of Moscow. Funds were raised here for the construction of Russia's first shrine to Our Lady of Fatima, built in St. Petersburg in 1997.

The National Marian Congress, held the third weekend in June, draws thousands with its focus on the call of the family to holiness.

SCHEDULE OF MASSES

Sunday: 7:30 a.m., Carmel Chapel; 9:30 a.m., Shrine Church
Daily: 7:30 a.m.
Confessions: Saturday, 7:00–8:00 p.m., Sunday, 9:00 a.m.

FACILITIES

Outdoor Shrine and Stations of the Cross
Bookstore

The House of Mary Shrine, Holy Innocents Memorial

DIOCESE OF SIOUX FALLS

LEWIS AND CLARK LAKE • YANKTON, SD 57078 • (605) 239-4532

HISTORY OF THE SHRINE

 The House of Mary Shrine was started in 1971 by a group of interested lay people in order to honor Mary, the Mother of God. It has always had the approval and blessing of the bishop.

The shrine is located on fifty acres of land on the Lewis and Clark Lake by Yankton, S.D. The lake attracts people from all over the country and the world.

The shrine has a Chapel of St. Joseph, where Masses are celebrated. A statue of Mary is on the hillside by the Rosary of Roses. Stations of the Cross wind up the hill to the three large crosses on the top of the hill. The meditation area, a quiet place for contemplative prayer, includes statues of St. Michael the Archangel and Moses with the Ten Commandments.

The grounds also contain small shrines to popular saints such as St. Teresa, St. Francis of Assisi, St. Benedictine, St. Isidore, along with a small memorial shrine to the Holy Innocents. Four hermitages in the wooded area are open for retreats and quiet praying.

The Sacred Heart Pond, blessed and dedicated by the bishop to the Sacred Heart of Jesus and Immaculate Heart of Mary, has a rosary made from stones around it. Pilgrims frequently pray this rosary.

SCHEDULE OF MASSES

Sunday: 1:00–4:50 p.m. (Adoration of the Blessed Sacrament, Chapel of St. Joseph)
First Saturday: 9:00 a.m. (Mass of the Blessed Virgin Mary, Chapel of St. Joseph);
    8:00 a.m., 15-Decade Rosary

DEVOTIONS

Rosary: Sunday, 4:00 p.m. (Chapel of St. Joseph)
Sunday: Marian Prayer Group 3:00–4:00 p.m.

Easter Sunday Sunrise Service (all faiths welcome) Prayers, Hymns, and Scripture
First Sunday in May: May Crowning of Mary
First Sunday in October: Respect for Life Rosary Rally (candlelight)
December 28: Holy Innocents (Prayers for reparation of murders by abortion, Chapel of St. Joseph)
Frequent Pilgrimages. Mass is celebrated in the Chapel of St. Joseph. (Reservations required; pilgrims must bring their own priest.)

The shrine is open year-round.

Dickeyville Grotto

DIOCESE OF MADISON
BOX 429 • 3305 W. MAIN STREET • DICKEYVILLE, WI 53808
(608) 568-7519 • (608) 568-8119

HISTORY OF THE SHRINE

 Fr. Mathias Wernerus built the grotto between 1920 and 1930. The dedication took place on September 14, 1930. The grotto is made up of several shrines, gardens, and fences. Made of stone, mortar, and brightly colored objects from around the world, it is dedicated to the unity of two great American ideals—love of God and love of country. The grotto was the creation of Fr. Mathias who used pieces of glass, gems, pottery, shells, fossils, corals, quartz, agates, and ores, among other materials, to piece his design together.

The grotto contains a statue of Our Lady and the Infant Jesus. On the outside walls, the Seven Gifts and the Twelve Fruits of the Holy Ghost are represented. The little shrine serves as a repository altar for the Corpus Christi Procession.

Approximately forty thousand people visit the grotto annually.

SCHEDULE OF MASSES
Sunday Vigil: 4:00 p.m., 8:00 p.m.
Sunday: 8:00 a.m., 10:00 a.m.
Holy Day of Obligation: 8:15 a.m., 5:30 p.m., 8:00 p.m.
Confessions: Saturday, 3:15 p.m.

DEVOTIONS
Novenas: Weekly
Rosary: Daily
Bible Class: Weekly

FACILITIES
Religious Bookstore
Gift Shop (April 1–October 31)
Guided Tours: Daily (June–August); Weekends (May, September, October)

Holy Hill—
Mary Help of Christians

ARCHDIOCESE OF MILWAUKEE
1525 CARMEL ROAD • HUBERTUS, WI 53033 • (414) 628-1838

HISTORY OF THE SHRINE

According to the stories of the Indians, Marquette erected a cross on the peak of what is now known as Holy Hill. The Irish heard of the story from the Catholic Indians, and, in 1855, Fr. Francis Paulhuber, pastor of an Irish parish in Goldendale, Wis., purchased the property. Three years later, he raised and blessed a 15-foot wooden cross there.

Because of the growing number of people making pilgrimages to Holy Hill, a small chapel was constructed and dedicated to Mary Help of Christians in 1863. This chapel housed the shrine statue, which was purchased in 1876 and brought to Holy Hill two years later. The day the statue arrived, it was carried in procession by eighteen young girls, escorted by horsemen and pilgrims, from St. Hubert's in Hubertus, Wis., a small town eight miles east of Holy Hill.

The popularity of Holy Hill as a place of pilgrimage continued to grow, and it soon became necessary to build a larger chapel. This chapel was dedicated by Archbishop Michael Heiss of Milwaukee in 1881. In 1906, Archbishop Sebastian Gebhard Messmer invited the Discalced Carmelites of Bavaria to staff the shrine. The Carmelites accepted the invitation and sent several of their order to establish a monastery there. A new church of Romanesque design was dedicated in 1931, and an adjoining monastery was added seven years later.

SCHEDULE OF MASSES

Sunday Vigil: 4:30 p.m.
Sunday: 8:00 a.m., 9:30 a.m., 11:00 a.m., 12:30 p.m.
Daily: Monday–Saturday, 6:00 a.m., 11:00 a.m.
Holy Day of Obligation: 6:00 a.m. and 11:00 a.m.
Healing Mass: fourth Sunday of each month
Confessions: 30 minutes before every Mass and upon request

DEVOTIONS

Novena: Monthly
Marian Devotions: Sunday, 2:30 p.m.
Rosary: Before the 11:00 a.m. Mass (May–October)
Stations of the Cross: Weekly during Lent
Sacred Concerts: Seasonally
Group Pilgrimages upon request

FACILITIES

Religious Bookstore/Gift Shop
Old Monastery Inn (Cafeteria)
Overnight Accommodations

Shrine of
Our Lady of Good Help

DIOCESE OF GREEN BAY
4047 CHAPEL DRIVE • NEW FRANKEN, WI 54129 • (414) 866-2571

HISTORY OF THE SHRINE

The shrine is devoutly called by many "The Chapel." The first log chapel was built in 1858 to enclose the spot where Mary allegedly appeared to Adele Brice. This chapel was replaced by a larger structure in 1861, which served until 1880. Ever increasing devotion to the Mother of God was heightened by the miraculous preservation of the chapel and its grounds from the encircling, devastating Peshtigo fire. Hence, a larger chapel was built in 1880. When this chapel was razed in 1941 to permit the erection of the present chapel, the two stumps of trees where Mary had appeared were found beneath the floor of the crypt. A statue of Mary with hands extended now occupies this spot. Bishop Paul Rhode dedicated the present chapel in 1942.

The ground floor of the chapel is used for the celebration of Mass and for private devotions. The spacious sanctuary graced with a large statute of Mary enables the devout to circle in a rosary pilgrimage. The crypt below is greatly venerated as the statue of Mary recalls the scene of the alleged apparitions of 1858.

The chapel is open daily.

SCHEDULE OF MASSES
Tuesday: 9:00 a.m.
August 15: 10:30 a.m.

DEVOTIONS
Holy Hour: Sunday, 2:30 p.m.

Northeast

Lourdes in Litchfield

ARCHDIOCESE OF HARTFORD
ROUTE 118 (EAST STREET) • P.O. BOX 667 • LITCHFIELD, CT 06759 • (860) 567-1041

HISTORY OF THE SHRINE

The shrine to Our Lady of Lourdes was built on the property of the Missionaries of the Company of Mary during the 1955 Marian Year. In the spirit of their founder, St. Louis de Montfort, the Missionaries welcome pilgrimages to this healing and peaceful place. Pilgrims are encouraged, in the context of a day of prayer, to renew their baptismal commitment, following Jesus Christ for *God Alone.*

SCHEDULE OF MASSES

Sunday: 11:30 a.m.
Tuesday–Saturday: 11:30 a.m.
Confessions: daily, upon request

DEVOTIONS

Way of the Cross: Sunday, 1:30 p.m., and on days of pilgrimage
Prayer: Sunday, 3:00 p.m., and on days of pilgrimage
Triduum: August 12–14, in preparation for the Feast of the Assumption, August 15
Anointing of Sick: May–October, one Sunday a month (call for schedule)
Blessing of Motorcycles: Third Sunday in May
Family Nights: One Friday a month (call for schedule)
Holy Hours: Fourth Tuesday, 7:00 p.m. in the Grotto
Pilgrimages and Retreats: Schedule with the shrine director

FACILITIES

Montfort Retreat House
Grotto
Book and Gift Shop
Cafeteria

LANGUAGES

English, Spanish, French, Italian, and Indonesian

La Salette Shrine

DIOCESE OF FALL RIVER
947 PARK STREET (ROUTE 118) • ATTLEBORO, MA 02703
(508) 222-5410 • FAX (508) 222-6770

HISTORY OF THE SHRINE

The shrine was officially opened on December 8, 1953 (the first day of the Marian Year) with the first Christmas Festival of Lights. The shrine keeps alive the memory of Mary's tearful apparition on the mountain of La Salette, in France, on September 19, 1946. The focus of the shrine ministries is reconciliation—the core of Mary's message at La Salette and the charism of the La Salette Missionaries.

Important celebrations include the La Salette Triduum; Divine Mercy Sunday; Catholic Tent Revival; Christmas Festival of Lights; Pilgrimage Day for People with Disabilities; Evangelization of Youth; and Ethnic Pilgrimage Days for Filipinos, Hispanics, Vietnamese, Haitians, Poles, Franco-Americans, and Portuguese.

SCHEDULE OF MASSES

Sunday Vigil: 4:30 p.m.
Sunday: 12:10 p.m.
Daily: 12:10 p.m.; Monday–Friday, 6:30 p.m.
Holy Day of Obligation Vigil: 6:30 p.m.
Holy Day of Obligation: 12:10 p.m.
Confessions: Monday–Friday, 2:00–3:00 p.m., 5:00–6:00 p.m.;
    Saturday, 1:00-4:00 p.m.; Sunday, 1:00–5:00 p.m.

DEVOTIONS

Rosary: Weekdays, 11:45 p.m., 6:00 p.m.
Healing Service: Sunday, 2:00 p.m.
Padre Pio Prayer Group: Monday, 7:15 p.m.
La Salette Novena: Wednesday, 12:10 p.m., 6:30 p.m..
La Salette and Divine Mercy Devotions: Wednesday, 7:15 p.m.
Bible Class: Wednesday
La Salette Prayer Group: Thursday, 7:30 p.m.
Retreats: Year-round

FACILITIES
Indoor and Outdoor Chapels
Theater
Garden of the Apparition
Rosary Walk
Religious Bookstore
Counseling Center
Gift Shop
Cafeteria
Retreat House

LANGUAGES
English, French, Portuguese, and Spanish

St. Clement's Eucharistic Shrine

ARCHDIOCESE OF BOSTON
1105 BOYLSTON STREET • BOSTON, MA 02215 • (617) 266-5999
(Located in downtown Boston. Easily accessible by car or the "T," the city's subway system.)

HISTORY OF THE SHRINE

St. Clement Eucharistic Shrine was established May 3, 1945, by the late Cardinal Richard J. Cushing, as the official Archdiocesan Shrine for Eucharistic Adoration. The shrine is intended to be a center for worship and growth in the mystery of the eucharist; it provides a prayerful atmosphere for the Adoration of the Blessed Sacrament exposed.

St. Clement Eucharistic Shrine is staffed by the Oblates of the Virgin Mary. This shrine also serves as their house of formation and seminary for those preparing for the priesthood and religious life as Oblates.

SCHEDULE OF MASSES

Saturday: 11:00 a.m.
Sunday: 11:00 a.m.
Weekday: 7:00 a.m., 12:10 p.m.
Holy Day of Obligation: Regular schedule
Easter Triduum: Please call the church office
Confessions: Saturday and Sunday, before the scheduled Mass
Confession and spiritual direction are also offered by appointment.

DEVOTIONS

Rosary: 5:30 p.m. followed by Evening Prayer
Exposition of the Blessed Sacrament: Monday–Friday, 5:30–8:45 p.m.; Saturday and Sunday, following the celebration of the Eucharist: 6:00 p.m. Exposition ends with the rite of Benediction.
Nocturnal Adoration: First Friday of each month. (Please note: We will also be very happy to provide Eucharistic Adoration for groups planning a visit. Please call us in advance.)

FACILITIES

The Oblates of the Virgin Mary devote themselves to the spiritual formation of the clergy and laity. For groups seeking a day of recollection, St. Clement's offers facilities including parking, meeting areas, library, and other needs according to the groups. Please contact us with any questions.

LANGUAGES

English, Italian, and Spanish

Madonna, Queen of the Universe National Shrine

ARCHDIOCESE OF BOSTON
111 ORIENT AVENUE • EAST BOSTON, MA 02128 • (617) 569-2100 • FAX (617) 561-1138

HISTORY OF THE SHRINE

The Madonna Queen of the Universe National Shrine was founded in 1954 and is conducted by the Don Orione Fathers, a religious congregation of Italian origin. The 35-foot statue of the Blessed Mother venerated here was created by the renowned Italian-Jewish sculptor, Arrigo Minerbi, and is a replica of one that stands on top of Monte Mario in Rome.

On December 8, 1943, Minerbi, fleeing from the Nazis, was given refuge in the houses of the Don Orione Fathers in Rome, where he remained until the war ended. As a personal act of thanksgiving and to fulfill a vow made by the people of Rome to the Blessed Mother, Minerbi agreed to create a statue of Mary.

When the friends and benefactors of the nascent works of charity of Don Orione in the States saw the completed statue in Rome, they asked Minerbi to make another one for Boston. In this way, they sought to fulfill the desire of Don Orione himself that beside every work of charity (in this particular case the Nursing Home for the Elderly) there would be a work of faith. Cardinal Richard J. Cushing gave his full approval for the erection of a shrine to Our Blessed Lady and suggested the title "Queen of the Universe" in keeping with the 1950 proclamation of the dogma of the Assumption of Mary.

Throughout the years, the Madonna Shrine has been a popular landmark for visitors to Boston and a point of reference and refreshment in the lives of the many people who come again and again to seek Mary's powerful intercession.

SCHEDULE OF MASSES
Sunday Vigil: 7:30 p.m.
Sunday: 11:00 a.m., 4:30 p.m.
Weekdays: 8:30 a.m., 7:30 p.m.
Holy Day of Obligation Vigil: 7:30 p.m.
Holy Day of Obligation: 8:30 a.m., 7:30 p.m.
Confessions: Before all Masses; Saturday, 6:30 p.m., 7:20 p.m.
Special Masses for groups may be arranged

DEVOTIONS
Holy Rosary: Weekdays, 7:00 p.m.; Sundays, 3:30 p.m.
Evening Prayer and Benediction: Sunday, 3:45 p.m.
Holy Hour for Vocations: First Thursday of the Month, 8:00 p.m.
First Saturday Devotions: First Saturday of the Month, 8:30 a.m.

NOVENAS
Immaculate Conception: November 29–December 7, 7:00 p.m.
Christmas: December 16– 23, 7:00 p.m.

ANNUAL CELEBRATIONS
Blessed Louis Orione, Founder: March 12
Annual May Procession: Last Sunday in May, 7:00 p.m.
Madonna, Queen of the Universe: Last Sunday in August, 3:00 p.m.
Dedication of the Shrine: November 29, 4:30 p.m.

FACILITIES
Days of Recollection and Retreats (available on request)
Gift Shop
Catholic Adult Education Courses
Large Pilgrim Reception Center
Accessible to people with disabilities
*Reasonably priced meals for groups at the shrine may be arranged in advance.

LANGUAGES
English, Spanish, and Italian

St. Anne Shrine

DIOCESE OF WORCESTER
16 CHURCH STREET • FISKDALE, MA 01518 • (508) 347-7338

HISTORY OF THE SHRINE

The parish was formed by the union of two missions in 1887. In that year, on the Sunday following the Feast of St. Anne, a parishioner was partially healed of a physical ailment in the church. The following year, on the same Sunday, she was completely healed. Parishioners then gathered at the church and formed the first procession in thanksgiving to God for this favor obtained through the intercession of St. Anne. With that celebration, the shrine was born.

An authentic relic of St. Anne was donated to the Sturbridge shrine in 1893. An outdoor chapel was built, and Sunday Masses began to be celebrated outside. In 1955, Bishop John J. Wright entrusted the care of the shrine to the Assumptionists. In 1971, the Assumptionists brought their unique collection of Russian icons to the shrine for public viewing.

Since that first healing more than one hundred years ago, people have continued to come to this holy place to seek solace and peace from God through the intercession of St. Anne.

SCHEDULE OF MASSES
Sunday Vigil: 4:00 p.m.
Sunday: 8:00 a.m., 10:00 a.m., noon, 6:00 p.m.
Monday–Friday: 7:30 a.m., 9:30 a.m.
Saturday: 7:30 a.m.
Holy Day of Obligation Vigil: 7:00 p.m.
Holy Day of Obligation: 7:30 a.m., 9:30 a.m., 7:00 p.m.
Confessions: Saturday, 2:30 p.m., 7:00 p.m.; and upon request

DEVOTIONS
Annual Novena, July 18–July 26

FACILITIES

Votive Shrine
Votive Chapel
Icon Chapel
Way of the Cross
Lourdes Grotto
Holy Stairs to Life-Sized Crucifix
Outdoor Mass Pavilion (weekend Masses Memorial Day–Labor Day: weather permitting)
Gift Shop
Bookstore
Picnic Grove

LANGUAGES

English and French

Our Lady of Fatima Shrine

ARCHDIOCESE OF BOSTON
101 SUMMER STREET • HOLLISTON, MA 01746 • (508) 429-2144

HISTORY OF THE SHRINE:

Our Lady of Fatima Shrine at Holliston, Mass., built and directed by the Xaverian Missionaries, is one of the leading centers of Marian devotion in New England. The purpose of the shrine is to make known the message of Our Lady of Fatima, a truly missionary message, and to offer a tranquil setting near the mission center where people can come to pray and to meditate.

Fatima Shrine was established by Fr. Henry Frassineti, a Xaverian priest who came to the United States after spending eighteen years as a missionary in China, where he built what is believed to be the first chapel in the world dedicated to Our Lady of Fatima.

The first Xaverian house was an abandoned farmhouse. The unkempt, swampy grounds were gradually transformed into a pleasant garden with hills, ponds, and winding paths. The Hill of Fatima, with the altar for the celebration of Mass, was the original shrine. Over the years it has been joined with many other public worship places such as Fatima, Stations of the Cross, *The Pieta*, Calvary, Rosary Walk, and so on.

The shrine is an inspiration to all visitors who seek a deeper spiritual life closer to Jesus through Mary, the Mother of God.

SCHEDULE OF MASSES
Sunday: 11:00 a.m.
Confessions: 3:00–5:00 p.m.; also upon request

DEVOTIONS
World Mission Rosary: Sunday, 3:00 p.m.
Bible Class: Fridays
Retreats: Weekly
Public Worship of the Blessed Sacrament: Sunday, 3:30 p.m.

FACILITIES
Religious Bookstore
Gift Shop
Counseling Center
Cultural Center
World Mission Rosary Makers

LANGUAGES
French, Italian, English, Spanish, Portuguese, and Japanese

St. Joseph the Worker Shrine

ARCHDIOCESE OF BOSTON
37 LEE STREET • BOX 1276 • LOWELL, MA 01853 • (508) 458-6346

HISTORY OF THE SHRINE

From a modest settlement of Indians and English settlers grouped at the junction of the Concord and Merrimack Rivers evolved in the nineteenth century the largest concentration of cotton and weaving mills in the hemisphere.

By 1836, the year of Lowell's incorporation, eight new mills started operation. In 1864, several manufacturers had commissioned Samuel P. Marin to visit his native Quebec Province to recruit labor for Lowell's mills. The Canadian response was overwhelming. As the number of Franco-Americans increased, so did the concern for their spiritual heritage and religious situation.

From 1866 to 1868, the Franco-American population of the Archdiocese of Boston had already doubled. Most Rev. John J. Williams desperately needed a French-speaking priest who could take up residence in Lowell for the spiritual needs of Franco-Canadian immigrants arriving in Lawrence, Lowell, Haverhill, Marlboro, and the Merrimack Valley.

In 1867, Archbishop Williams went to Burlington, Vt.; there he met a provincial of the Oblates of Mary Immaculate from Montreal, Canada. He made a most urgent plea for missionaries who could come to Lowell to form a French-speaking parish. The following year, two Oblate missionaries arrived in Lowell from Montreal.

Fr. Lucien Lagler, OMI, and Fr. Andre M. Garin, OMI, immediately began preaching a parish mission in the basement of St. Patrick's Church for the French-speaking population. The response was so overwhelming that Fr. Garin decided to purchase a church building from a society of spiritualists. The first Mass at the new site, held shortly afterward, was on the Feast of St. Joseph; Fr. Garin chose the saint as the patron for the parish.

St. Joseph's Church became the religious and social center of the Franco-American population. The lower level of the church served as halls for all sodalities and societies meetings. Recent immigrants from Canada looked for work and met on the church steps after the liturgy for interviews with bosses and employers of the Lowell mills.

The church was rededicated as the Shrine of St. Joseph, Patron of Workers, on May 10, 1956, by Archbishop Richard J. Cushing of Boston and Bishop Jean Louis Collignon, OMI, of the Diocese of Les Cayes, Haiti.

The shrine is open daily, 7:00 a.m.–6:00 p.m. and currently serves the sacramental needs of the Greater Lowell Metropolitan Area.

SCHEDULE OF MASSES
Sunday Vigil: 4:00 p.m., 5:30 p.m.
Sunday: 8:15 a.m., 10:15 a.m., 11:30 a.m.
Monday–Friday: 8:00 a.m., noon, 5:40 p.m.
Saturday: 8:00 a.m., noon, 4:00 p.m., 5:30 p.m.
Holy Day of Obligation Vigil: 5:30 p.m.
Holy Day of Obligation: 8:00 a.m., 5:40 p.m.
Confessions: Monday–Friday, 10:00 a.m.–12:55 p.m., 4:30–5:25 p.m.;
     Saturday, 10:00 a.m.–12:55 p.m.

DEVOTIONS
Rosary: Monday–Friday, Joyful Mysteries: 7:20 a.m.; Sorrowful Mysteries:11:40 a.m.;
     Glorious Mysteries: 5:10 p.m.
Morning Prayer: Monday–Friday, 7:45 a.m.
Exposition of the Blessed Sacrament: Monday–Saturday, 8:30 a.m.
Evening Prayer: Monday–Friday, 5:30 p.m.
Novenas: Wednesday (after all Masses): St. Joseph and St. Eugene de Mazenod

Basilica and Shrine of Our Lady of Perpetual Help

ARCHDIOCESE OF BOSTON
1545 TREMONT STREET • ROXBURY, MA 02120 • (617) 445-2600 • FAX (617) 445-1857

HISTORY OF THE SHRINE

In 1854, Pope Pius IX commissioned the Redemptorists to spread devotion to Our Lady of Perpetual Help, and he gave the original picture to their care; it is cherished in their church on Via Merulana in Rome. When the Basilica of Our Lady of Perpetual Help was constructed in 1871, a magnificent altar of Carrara marble, in honor of Our Lady of Perpetual Help, was built as its centerpiece. The church was named a basilica in 1954 by Pope Pius XII.

The basilica contains a beautiful picture of Our Mother of Perpetual Help, where many visitors have come to plead for favors. There is proof these favors are answered. Beneath the picture are two vases containing crutches, canes, and casts. The first recorded miracle at the shrine occurred on August 18, 1883, when a little crippled girl who was making a novena suddenly gave her crutches to her brother, thanked the Lord, and walked out of the church. More cures followed, and newspapers across the country hailed the mission church shrine as Lourdes in the land of the Puritans.

Today, more than one hundred years later, devotions in honor of the Mother of Perpetual Help are held at the shrine every Wednesday. The main celebrations of the year include Easter, the Feast of Our Lady of Perpetual Help, and the Feasts of St. Alphonsus and St. John Neumann. The shrine is staffed by the Redemptorists and the School Sisters of Notre Dame.

SCHEDULE OF MASSES
Sunday Vigil: 4:00 p.m.
Sunday: 8:00 a.m., 9:30 a.m., 11:00 a.m. (Spanish), 12:30 p.m., 6:30 p.m.
Daily: 7:00 a.m. (except Saturday), 8:00 a.m., 9:00 a.m., 12:10 p.m.
Holy Day of Obligation Vigil: 5:30 p.m.
Holy Day of Obligation: 7:00 a.m., 8:00 a.m., 9:00 a.m., 12:10 p.m., 5:30 p.m.,
    6:30 p.m. (Spanish)
Confessions: Saturday: 3:15–3:45 p.m.; and after all Masses

DEVOTIONS

Novenas: Wednesdays at Mass time, 7:00 a.m., 8:00 a.m., 9:00 a.m., 12:30 p.m., 6:30 p.m.; Outside of Mass time, 5:30 p.m., 7:30 p.m.
Rosary: Daily
Exposition of Blessed Sacrament: Friday, Sunday
Benediction: Wednesday, Friday, Sunday

FACILITIES

Counseling Center

LANGUAGES

English, Spanish, and Portuguese

The National Shrine of the Divine Mercy

DIOCESE OF SPRINGFIELD
EDEN HILL • P.O. BOX 951 • STOCKBRIDGE, MA 01262 • (413) 298-3931
E-MAIL: DMSHRINE@AOL.COM

HISTORY OF THE SHRINE

The National Shrine of the Divine Mercy is a popular pilgrimage site known for exquisite wood carvings and stained-glass windows. Erected in thanksgiving to the mercy of God, the shrine is a unique sanctuary of hope in a troubled world. Pilgrims have been drawn to Eden Hill since 1944 to implore God's Mercy. They have been drawn by the rays of Mercy and Love symbolized by the first Image of the Divine Mercy in the United States in a place of honor over the main altar. The interior of the shrine was dedicated in 1960. In the side altar on the right, a relic of Blessed Faustina Kowalska was enshrined by Cardinal Bernarad Law of Boston on August 8, 1993. Blessed Faustina was born in Poland in 1905 and was entrusted with the prophetic message of God's Mercy for our times in appearances of Our Lord to her in the 1930s. She died in 1938 and was beatified by Pope John Paul II in 1993.

The shrine offices are open daily 8:30 a.m.–5:00 p.m. Pilgrimages are welcomed all year (reservations required for groups). The shrine is staffed by the Marians of the Immaculate Conception and is located on 350 acres of land called Eden Hill. The shrine, shrine offices, and gift shop are easily accessible to people with special needs.

The shrine staff invites pilgrims to prepare for the celebration of the Great Jubilee 2000 and the Third Millennium by coming on pilgrimage to the National Shrine of the Divine Mercy over the next three years. A novena of teachings regarding the Great Jubilee will be held every fourth Monday of the month beginning in April, 7:00–8:30 p.m. Please call ahead for other Millennium programs and services.

SCHEDULE OF MASSES

Sunday: 10:30 a.m.
Daily: 2:00 p.m.
Saturday: 8:00 a.m.
Holy Day of Obligation: 8:00 a.m. (Call ahead)
Confessions: Daily, after the Chaplet of the Divine Mercy, 3:00 p.m.

DEVOTIONS
Perpetual Novena and the Chaplet of the Divine Mercy; Adoration and Benediction of the Most Blessed Sacrament; Veneration of the Relic of Blessed Faustina, Daily, 3:00 p.m.
Divine Mercy Sunday: First Sunday after Easter.

FACILITIES
Gift Shop, Monday–Saturday, 9:00 a.m.–5:00 p.m.; Sunday 9:00 a.m.–5:00 p.m. (Closed for 10:30 a.m. Mass)

LANGUAGES
English and Polish

Shrine of Our Lady of Grace

DIOCESE OF MANCHESTER
ROUTE 3 • COLEBROOK, NH 03576 • (603) 237-5511

HISTORY OF THE SHRINE

This shrine was established in 1948 as a glowing tribute of love and thanksgiving to Our Lady of Grace for the countless blessings that she bestowed on the Missionary Oblates of Mary Immaculate during their first twenty-five years in Colebrook, N.H.

To enhance the natural beauty of the site nestled between the White Mountains of N.H. and the Green Mountains of Vt., the Oblates used field stones as the primary construction materials of the 110' x 85' main monument with a 21' high pedestal on which stands an 8'2" Carrara marble statue of Our Lady of Grace. In 1952, a Permanent Altar in Rock of Ages granite was placed before this monument. An outdoor Way of the Cross in Stanhope, QC granite and Carrara marble was erected and the 15 Mysteries of the Rosary in Rock of Ages granite and Carrara marble were completed in 1954. A 130' x 90' replica of the Worldmission Rosary was built in 1955. A mountain-spring fed Family Rosary Lake was dedicated in 1958. A monument honoring Motorcyclists in Prayer was blessed in 1986, tenth anniversary of the annual motorcycle blessing.

The Shrine of Our Lady of Grace is a seasonal shrine open Mother's Day until the second Sunday of October.

SCHEDULE OF MASSES
Daily (including Sunday), 11:00 a.m.
Any hour to accommodate pilgrimage groups

DEVOTIONS
Rosary, Homily, and Benediction: Sunday, 3:00 p.m.
Mass, Holy Hour, Way of the Cross for pilgrimage groups
Confessions: Before each Mass and on request

SPECIAL EVENTS
Blessing of Motorcycles: Sunday after Father's Day
Assumption Triduum: August 13, 14, and 15

FACILITIES
Gift Shop
Picnic Areas
Rest Rooms

LANGUAGES
English and French

Shrine of Our Lady of La Salette

DIOCESE OF MANCHESTER

ROUTE 4-A • P.O. BOX 420 • ENFIELD, NH 03748 • (603) 632-7087 • FAX (603) 632-4301

HISTORY OF THE SHRINE

Founded in 1951, the Shrine of Our Lady of La Salette, near Lake Mascoma, N.H., is a place of prayer and meditation in a unique, natural setting of peace and beauty. On September 19, 1846, Mary, the Mother of God, appeared to two shepherd children on the slope of a mountain in the French Alps, near the village of La Salette, France. The "Beautiful Lady," as they called her, was seated on a stone, her elbows resting on her knees, her face buried in her hands, weeping bitterly. She rose, calming the children's fear by her reassuring look and maternal voice. She told them the cause of her tears: disobedience to the laws of God and of the Church, blasphemy, failure to keep the Lord's Day, and lack of prayer. On the shrine grounds are a replica of the apparition site at La Salette in France, a rosary pond, outdoor Stations of the Cross, the Calvary scene with Holy Stairs, and a peace walk. The shrine is open throughout the year.

The shrine is located in the midst of a historical Shaker Village, which also offers tours. Lodging and meals for groups and individuals are available in the area.

SCHEDULE OF MASSES

Sunday Vigil: 7:30 p.m.
Sunday: 11:00 a.m. (summer season)
Monday, Tuesday, Friday: 11:30 a.m.
Confessions: 30 minutes before Mass and upon request

DEVOTIONS

Varies according to seasonal schedule

FACILITIES

Pilgrim's Chapel
Reconciliation Chapel
Gift Shop
Book Shop
Facilities for Private Retreats

National Shrine of St. Gerard

ARCHDIOCESE OF NEWARK
ST. LUCY'S CHURCH • 118 SEVENTH AVENUE • NEWARK, NJ 07104 • (201) 482-6663

HISTORY OF THE SHRINE:

 In 1899, a small group from Caposele, Italy, introduced the feast devoted to St. Gerard Majella to the United States. This devotion began in St. Lucy's Parish, Newark, N.J., in 1899, five years before Gerard's canonization. The devotion grew steadily throughout the years, and in 1977, St. Gerard's chapel in St. Lucy's Church was dedicated as a national shrine by Archbishop Peter Gerety.

St. Gerard was born in Muro, a small town in the south of Italy, on April 6, 1726. Although he had frail health, he was accepted as a lay brother into the Congregation of the Most Holy Redeemer. During his apprenticeship he performed many miracles, and he is known especially for his "motherhood" miracles. Although he has not been officially designated as the patron of mothers, the title has been given to him by popular acclaim in many countries, including the United States. St. Gerard died in October 1755 at age 29. His feast day is October 16.

Each year during the parish feast days, which includes October 16, there are traditional lights, music, food stands, and processions. Also, the shrine is visited throughout the year by faithful seeking the intercession of St. Gerard.

DEVOTIONS:

Wednesday: 5:30 p.m. (Novena and Mass)
Novena and Mass: Nine days prior to the feast day of St. Gerard,
    October 16: 7:00 p.m.
Anointing of the Sick: On day seven of the novena
Blessing of Expectant Mothers: On day eight of the novena
Blessing of All Babies Born during the Year: On day nine of the novena
There are processions on the feast day of St. Gerard, as well as on the Saturday and
    Sunday closest to his feast day. This varies from year to year.

We will celebrate the one hudredth anniversary of the Annual Feast of St. Gerard at St. Lucy's Parish on October 16, 1999.

St. Joseph Shrine

DIOCESE OF PATERSON
1050 LONG HILL ROAD • STIRLING, NJ 07980 • (908) 647-0208

HISTORY OF THE SHRINE

The shrine was founded in 1924 by the founder of Missionary Servants of the Most Holy Trinity, Fr. Thomas Augustine Judge, for devotion to St. Joseph. It has served as a school and a retreat center and is now a place of retreat, pilgrimage, and spiritual refuge. Days of renewal are available for groups of twenty or more. There are no overnight retreats.

The two main celebrations of the year are the Feasts of St. Joseph and St. Anthony. There is also a one-week Korean Day Camp for children during the summer.

SCHEDULE OF MASSES

Daily: Monday, Wednesday, Friday, Saturday, 8:00 a.m.; Tuesday, Thursday, 5:30 p.m.
Holy Day of Obligation: 8:00 a.m., 10:00 a.m.
Confessions: Anytime

DEVOTIONS

Novenas: Annually
Rosary: Daily
Bible Class: Biannually
Novena to St. Joseph: Every Sunday

FACILITIES

Religious Bookstore
Gift Shop
Overnight Accommodations (for Religious only)

Rosary Shrine (Monastery of Our Lady of the Rosary)

ARCHDIOCESE OF NEWARK
543 SPRINGFIELD AVENUE • SUMMIT, NJ 07901 • (908) 273-1228

HISTORY OF THE SHRINE

Perpetual adoration of the eucharist and the rosary are the focal points of devotion at Rosary Shrine, the Monastery of the Dominican Nuns in Summit, N.J., which is primarily a sanctuary of prayer. Pilgrims can pay tribute to their eucharistic Lord, exposed day and night for their adoration, and can pray the rosary in company with the Mother of Jesus.

On May 22, 1921, a group of pilgrims from Paterson, N.J., traveled to the newly founded Monastery of Our Lady of the Rosary, where the first outdoor public rosary pilgrimage in the United States took place. On the occasion of the shrine's dedication, Pope Benedict XV sent an apostolic blessing granting a plenary indulgence to all the faithful who would participate in the pilgrimage.

Since that time, the shrine has become widely known and has drawn as many as fifteen thousand pilgrims during the May and October devotions, especially between 1923 and 1934. The privilege of perpetual exposition of the Most Blessed Sacrament was granted to the monastery on February 11, 1926, the Feast of Our Lady of Lourdes.

The monastery is noted for its replica of the Winding Sheet of Turin, which is said to be the cloth in which Our Blessed Lord was wrapped for burial. The replica was fully authenticated and approved by the late Bishop John J. O'Connor of Newark, who authorized its public veneration.

The shrine is the home of twenty-two Dominican Nuns, who spend their lives in giving glory to God and honor to his Mother.

SCHEDULE OF MASSES

Sunday: 7:30 a.m.
Weekdays: 7:15 a.m.
Holy Day of Obligation: 7:15 a.m.

DEVOTIONS

Coronation Pilgrimage: First Sunday of May: 3:00 p.m.
Rosary Pilgrimage: First Sunday of October: 3:00 p.m.
Eucharistic-Marian Hour: Semiannually
Perpetual Adoration of the Blessed Sacrament

FACILITIES

Gift Shop

National Blue Army Shrine of the Immaculate Heart of Mary

DIOCESE OF METUCHEN
P.O. BOX 976 • WASHINGTON, NJ 07882 • (908) 689-1700

HISTORY OF THE SHRINE

The National Blue Army Shrine of the Immaculate Heart of Mary was built in 1978 as a center for the promotion of the message of Our Lady of Fatima within the context of the Church's Marian doctrine and devotion. The shrine is administered by the Blue Army of Our Lady of Fatima, U.S.A., Inc. through its executive director. The shrine is staffed by the Oblates of the Virgin Mary and the Handmaids of Mary Immaculate.

On the thirteenth of each month, from May through October, the anniversary of the Fatima apparitions is celebrated beginning at noon. All-night vigils are held on the First Friday/First Saturday of each month throughout the year, beginning at 9:00 p.m. on Friday.

SCHEDULE OF MASSES

Thirteenth of each month, May–October, 1:30 p.m.
Daily: 11:30 a.m.
Latin Liturgy: First Sunday of the Month: 11:30 a.m.
Confessions: 20 minutes before Mass

DEVOTIONS

All-Night Vigil: First Friday/Saturday
Novenas: Annually
Rosary: Daily
Benediction: Daily
Exposition: Daily

FACILITIES

Religious Gift Shop
Outdoor Rosary Garden and Way of the Cross
Holy House, USA chapel (replica of Holy House of Loreto)
Picnic Tables
Capelinha (replica of Chapel at Fatima)
Reservations requested for groups of ten or more by car, van, or bus.
     Write or call for details.

Shrine of Our Lady of Martyrs

DIOCESE OF ALBANY
NOELTNER ROAD • AURIESVILLE, NY 12016 • (518) 853-3033

HISTORY OF THE SHRINE

The shrine was built in 1885 on the site of the martyrdoms of Saints Rene Goupil, Isaac Jogues, and John LaLande. It was named Our Lady of Martyrs with the approval of the bishops of the Third Council of Baltimore. After their beatification in 1925, it was also called the Jesuit Martyrs Shrine.

The main concern of the shrine apostolate is to promote devotion to Our Lady and martyrs. Pilgrims are provided with opportunities for reconciliation, fostering devotion, and strengthening their faith.

SCHEDULE OF MASSES

Sunday Vigil: 4:00 p.m.
Sunday: 9:00 a.m., 10:30 a.m., noon, 4:00 p.m.
Daily: 11:30 a.m., 4:00 p.m.
Holy Day of Obligation Vigil: 4:00 p.m.
Holy Day of Obligation: 11:30 a.m., 4:00 p.m.
Confessions: Before Mass each day; priests are available 10:00 a.m.–4:30 p.m.

DEVOTIONS

Novenas: Eight held annually
Rosary: Daily after 11:30 Mass
Benediction and Blessing with Relics: Daily, 3:30 p.m.
Stations of the Cross: Sunday, 2:30 p.m.

FACILITIES

Religious Bookstore
Counseling Center
Gift Shop
Cafeteria
Cultural Center

Sacred Heart Diocesan Shrine

DIOCESE OF BUFFALO
5337 GENESEE STREET • ROUTE 31 • BOWMANSVILLE, NY 14026 • (716) 683-2375

HISTORY OF THE SHRINE

The present Sacred Heart Diocesan Shrine consists of a large fieldstone shrine one-and-one-half stories high, built by the men of the parish in 1926 (Immaculate Conception portion) and 1927 (Sacred Heart portion), in a park-like setting.

The first (main) part of the shrine is dedicated to the Eucharistic Heart of Jesus and contains three arches designed to recall the Blessed Trinity. A Last Supper scene and a crucifix, both made from Italian marble, recall the eucharist. The crucifix depicts a heart on Christ's chest and recalls his Gospel of Love, further given to us through Calvary and each eucharist. Thirty-three steps, representing the number of years of Christ's life, lead above the shrine to a statue of Christ the King; the statue also depicts a heart on his chest.

The second portion of the shrine is dedicated to the Immaculate Conception of the Blessed Virgin Mary. Built in the form of a heart through which the worshiper enters, the shrine contains marble statues of the Annunciation, the apparition at Lourdes, and the Assumption.

A fountain, from which water flows down the face of the shrine, recalls the many miracles that occurred at Lourdes through its waters and through faith. At the top rear portion of the heart, an image of the Sorrowful Mother represents the hard aspects of life made bearable through the abundant grace of God, especially as given in his sacraments. (A Man of Sorrows is displayed in the Sacred Heart Shrine.)

The outdoor shrine also contains altars in honor of St. Joseph, St. Anthony, and the Little Flower; there are outdoor Stations of the Cross as well.

A statue showing the Lord offering the host and chalice as in the Mass was placed over the church altar in 1954. A special statue, used during the thirtieth anniversary of the apparitions at Fatima, carved by the same sculptor as the Eucharistic Christ statue, is located at the side altar. Carved wooden Stations of the Cross came from Ortiese, Italy; a large carved crucifix came from Oberammergau, Germany. Other carvings at the shrine were created by the Lippich brothers, who resided in

Bowmansville. A "children's corner" was created with the kneeler, height of artwork, and so forth designed for use by children only. Fine stained-glass windows stress the missionary character of the church and the time-tested devotions of the Church.

Many local war veterans are buried in the cemetery in the woods behind the school. The large crucifix in the center is from Switzerland.

SCHEDULE OF MASSES
Sunday Vigil: 6:30 p.m.
Sunday: 7:45 a.m., 9:00 a.m., 12:15 p.m.
First Friday: 9:00 a.m., 7:30 p.m.
Holy Day of Obligation: 7:00 a.m., 9:00 a.m., 11:00 a.m., 6:30 p.m.
Confessions: Saturday, 3:30–5:30 p.m., 7:15–8:00 p.m.; and upon request

DEVOTIONS
First Friday Mass and Devotions: 9:30 a.m., 7:30 p.m.followed by Holy Hour.
First Saturday Mass, Rosary and Holy Hour: 8:00 p.m.
Solemnity of the Sacred Heart, preceeded by Triduum
May Crowning
Memorial Day Mass: 11:00 a.m. (cemetery)
July: Living Rosary

Our Lady, Help of Christians Shrine

DIOCESE OF BUFFALO

4125 UNION ROAD • CHEEKTOWAGA, NY 14225 • (716) 634-3420

HISTORY OF THE SHRINE

This is truly an immigrant shrine. The family of Joseph Batt left Alsace in 1836. On the voyage across the Atlantic, when a terrible storm snapped the masts of the ship, the Batts urgently begged the immediate assistance of Our Lady, Help of Christians, while the crew chopped the ropes and masts that almost capsized the ship. Joseph promised to build a shrine to Our Lady if the family survived. The craft survived the storm but drifted without sails; the Gulf Stream brought them to the Irish coast.

True to his promise, Joseph built a small shrine in 1853. Additions were made as immigrants learned about the shrine and came to pray for their urgent needs. The oldest shrine in western New York, this shrine continues in popularity, especially on the Solemnity of the Assumption, August 14.

The old church once displayed many crutches, canes, and so forth, along the walls, testifying to the many favors received through the intercession of Our Lady, Help of Christians. These were removed to create more room for worshipers before the parish could afford a new church. The Batts are buried in the cemetery behind the old church.

Over the altar, the original painting of the shrine pictures Our Lady with the Christ Child looking in concern upon the foundering ship containing the Batts during the storm. Early worshipers knew the shrine by the name "Maria Hilf (Mary Help) zu Cheektowaga, N.Y." The old church is on the National Register of Historic Places.

A large outdoor shrine of fieldstone features a Way of the Cross up to a Calvary scene; several altars are built within this stone structure. A stone sanctuary kept the priest dry during outdoor Masses in inclement weather. A Mother of Sorrows statue contains various personal memorabilia from pilgrims who take off their shoes for the last mile when walking here. At one time, many people walked from a far-off trolley stop to the shrine. A contemporary church features a woodcarving of Our Lady with a ship in her hand. The church also has a very fine organ.

SCHEDULE OF MASSES

Sunday Vigil: 4:00 p.m., 7:00 p.m.
Sunday: 7:00 a.m., 8:30 a.m., 10:00 a.m., noon
Holy Day of Obligation Vigil: 4:00 p.m., 7:00 p.m.
Holy Day of Obligation: 7:00 a.m., 8:30 a.m., 10:00 a.m., noon
Confessions: Saturday, 2:00–3:00 p.m.

DEVOTIONS

Miraculous Medal Novena: Wednesday, 9:30 a.m. (old church)
Solemnity of the Assumption: August 14

National Shrine of Blessed Kateri Tekakwitha

DIOCESE OF ALBANY
P.O. BOX 627 • FONDA, NY 12068 • (518) 853-3646

HISTORY OF THE SHRINE

Kateri Tekakwitha, an Indian maiden, was born on the Auriesville side of the Mohawk River in New York, to an Algonquin Indian mother and a Mohawk Indian chief. A few years later, a smallpox epidemic took the lives of her mother, father, and brother; it left her with weak eyes and pockmarked skin. In 1666, a French-and-Indian war party from Canada burned down all the Mohawk Indian villages, forcing the Mohawks to move to the Fonda side of the river. Kateri lived there for ten years in a village called Caughnawaga and was baptized a Christian by a Jesuit in 1676.

After conversion, Kateri refused marriage, preferring to devote her life completely to the Great Spirit and her people. The abuse she endured for her virtuousness drove her to seek refuge with the Christian Indians in Canada. There she became the first American Indian to take a vow of perpetual chastity. She died there in 1680 at the age of 24. It is documented that, at the moment of death, the pockmarks disappeared from her face.

In 1950, Kateri's village was discovered by a Conventual Franciscan, Fr. Thomas Grassman. He is responsible for excavating what is today the only completely excavated Mohawk Indian village in the country. Fr. Grassman was the shrine's first director, and it was he who saw to the shrine's growth until his death in 1970. The shrine was not considered to be an official place of devotion until Kateri was declared Blessed by Pope John Paul II in 1980. Blessed Kateri is the patroness of peace and ecology.

SCHEDULE OF MASSES
Sunday Vigil: 4:30 p.m. (outdoor pavilion)
Sunday: 10:00 a.m.
Daily: 8:00 a.m. (July–September)

DEVOTIONS
Feast Day of Kateri Tekakwitha: July 14

FACILITIES
Gift Shop
Retreat House
Nature Trails
Picnic Area
Fully Excavated Seventeenth-Century Mohawk Village
Native American Museum

Graymoor Christian Unity Center

ARCHDIOCESE OF NEW YORK
GARRISON, NY 10524 • (914) 424-3671

HISTORY OF THE SHRINE

 The center was established and is staffed by the Franciscan Order. The Franciscan Friars of the Atonement are well known for their work in Christian unity and for their missionary efforts around the world. This young community of men and women was founded in the Episcopal Church by Fr. Paul Wattson and Mother Lurana White in 1898 and was received into the Roman Catholic Church in 1909.

The unprecedented move of a group of religious people to be received together into the Catholic Church captured the imagination of people of both faiths. From the Mount of the Atonement, the magazine called *The Lamp*, along with the religious radio program *The Ave Maria Hour*, brought the message of unity and a growth in vocations to the new religious order. St. Christopher's Inn, a temporary shelter for homeless men, still attests to the missionary zeal of the founders, and many other ventures soon gave evidence of the spiritual sincerity of the small group of Franciscan Friars and Sisters at Graymoor, Garrison, N.Y., in the Hudson Valley.

Less than one hundred years later, the friars now serve the people of God in Japan, Brazil, England, Italy, Canada, and the United States.

SCHEDULE OF MASSES
Sunday: 10:00 a.m., 11:00 a.m.
Holy Day of Obligation: 8:00 a.m. (Community Mass)
Confessions: 9:00 a.m., 9:00 p.m.

DEVOTIONS
Bible Class: Weekly
Retreats: Weekly

FACILITIES
Religious Bookstore
Gift Shop
Overnight Accommodations (for retreats only)

Our Lady of Victory Basilica and National Shrine

DIOCESE OF BUFFALO
767 RIDGE ROAD • LACKAWANNA, NY 14218 • (716) 828-9444

HISTORY OF THE SHRINE

The Servant of God, Fr. Nelson R. Baker, spent all but one year of his long priestly life (1876–1936) caring for orphans, troubled youth, youthful offenders, unwed mothers and their offspring. He started with a few dozen youth; at times he cared for up to 1,000. His pro-life activities led him to build an infant home and maternity hospital and to expand the facilities continually. During the Depression, he and the Brothers of the Holy Infancy fed thousands. Students in the trade school mended thousands of pieces of clothing and as many pairs of shoes. Many African Americans were drawn to the church by Fr. Baker's defense of civil rights and because the church fed and clothed people in need. During this time, he served as vicar general to several bishops. The buildings on the opposite side of the street are evidence of the larger "City of Charity" Providence asked him to serve.

Our Lady of Victory National Shrine stands as a source of inspiration on Victory Hill. Under the leadership of Fr. Nelson Baker, who was devoted to Our Lady of Victory, the basilica was constructed in 1921 and was consecrated on May 25, 1926 by Cardinal Patrick Hayes. Two months later, Pope Pius XI elevated the shrine to a minor basilica, the second in the United States.

The architectural splendor of the shrine, which is reminiscent of the great European churches built during the Renaissance, fosters a prayerful atmosphere. The main altar is accented by twisted, red columns of rare Pyrenees marble and a nine-foot, 1,600-pound statue of Our Lady of Victory. The great center dome depicts the Coronation of Our Lady as Queen of Heaven and Earth.

The parish community of Our Lady of Victory welcomes pilgrims and visitors of all faiths.

SCHEDULE OF MASSES
Sunday Vigil: 4:30 p.m.
Sunday: 8:00 a.m., 10:00 a.m., noon, 4:30 p.m.
Weekday: 7:30 a.m., 8:30 a.m., 12:10 p.m.
Tuesday: 7:30 p.m.; followed by Charismatic prayer meeting
Holy Day of Obligation Vigil: 7:30 p.m.
Holy Day of Obligation: 7:30 a.m., 9:00 a.m., 12:10 p.m., 4:30 p.m.

DEVOTIONS
Rosary: Tuesday, 7:00 p.m.
Adoration of the Blessed Sacrament: Friday, 1:00 p.m.–midnight

NOVENAS
February 3–11: Novena of Masses for the Sick
March 11–19: In Honor of St. Joseph
May 16–24: In Honor of Our Lady of Victory
July 8–16: Thanksgiving to Our Lady of Victory
August 7–15: In Honor of Our Lady's Assumption
September 29–October 7: In Honor of Our Lady of Victory
November 1–30: A Month of Special Prayers for the Faithful Departed
December 17–25: In Honor of the Birth of Our Lord

FACILITIES
Gift Shop: 10:00 a.m.–4:00 p.m.
Small Museum: 10:00 a.m.–4:00 p.m.

National Shrine of Our Lady of Mount Carmel

ARCHDIOCESE OF NEW YORK
P.O. BOX 868 • CARMELITE DRIVE • MIDDLETOWN, NY 10940-0868
(914) 344-0876 • FAX (914) 344-0093
INTERNET: HTTP://WWW.MIDDLETOWN.NY.FRONTIERCOMM.NET/
E-MAIL: NSOLMC@NY.FRONTIERCOMM.NET

HISTORY OF THE SHRINE

Devotion to Mary under the title of Our Lady of Mount Carmel began more than eight hundred years ago in the Holy Land. From the beginning, the first Carmelites found in Mary a model for their own lives. Mary shared with the Carmelites, and they with the world, her scapular, a symbol of reconciliation.

The Carmelite devotion to Mary is shared with the world and serves to remind us that Mary was the first disciple of Jesus. As the model of Christian life, she is our teacher, a woman of the people who leads us to Christ.

The National Shrine of Our Lady of Mount Carmel was established in 1940 at the Carmelite Church of Our Lady of the Scapular of Mount Carmel at 28th Street and First Avenue in New York City. Part of the important work was to supply scapulars to the Armed Forces during World War II. The devotion to Our Lady of Mount Carmel grew at the shrine, and soon the work included days of reconciliation and workshops devoted to Mary. Thus began a full Marian Center with Masses, novenas, lectures, and study days.

In 1990, the shrine was transferred to Middletown, N.Y., where the beauty of the grounds, a magnificent chapel, and geographic location make it an ideal place for prayer, study, reflection, and pilgrimage. The shrine continues to offer daily and Sunday liturgies, days of recollection, novenas, and celebrations for special Carmelite feast days, rosary processions, sacrament of reconciliation, and spiritual direction. All programs at the National Shrine of Our Lady of Mount Carmel are conducted in English or Spanish and promote spirituality of prayer, reflection, meditation, and devotion to Mary. Special programs will be offered in 1997, 1998, and 1999 in preparation for the Third Millennium Jubilee in the year 2000.

SCHEDULE OF MASSES

Sunday: noon
Monday–Friday: 11:30 a.m.
Saturday: 11:30 a.m. for group pilgrimages upon request

DEVOTIONS

Special celebrations and novenas of Masses honoring Our Lady of Mount Carmel;
St. Therese; Carmelite Saints; Infant of Prague, St. Patrick
Special Liturgies during Advent and Lent.

FACILITIES

Large Shrine Chapel
Pilgrim Dining Hall
Meeting Rooms
Gift Shop

LANGUAGES

English and Spanish

St. Frances Cabrini Chapel

ARCHDIOCESE OF NEW YORK
701 FORT WASHINGTON AVENUE • NEW YORK, NY 10040 • (212) 923-3536

HISTORY OF THE SHRINE

The chapel was built in 1959 as a shrine for Mother Cabrini's body, which was moved here from Mother Cabrini High School in 1959. The body had been brought to the school chapel in 1933 from West Park, N.Y. In 1938, in the performance of rites necessary for beatification, the body was again exhumed and was transferred to a crystal coffin under the main altar of the sanctuary. On January 11, 1944, Pope Pius XII signed the Decree of Canonization of Blessed Frances Xavier Cabrini.

The remains of Mother Cabrini are enclosed in a glass coffin under the main altar of the chapel. Many visit daily to request graces, favors, and miracles because she has such great favor with God.

Groups may arrange a pilgrimage tour to the shrine which could include a talk and video, Mass, or a prayer service. The Blessed Sacrament is reserved in an adjoining chapel for those who wish to pray privately. A small photo exhibit depicting St. Cabrini and the works in which her Missionary Sisters of the Sacred Heart have engaged is located in the gift shop. The shrine is open every day from 9:00 a.m. to 4:30 p.m. (except major holidays).

St. Cabrini's feast day is November 13. The shrine celebrates her feast during the second weekend of November with seven masses in five languages.

SCHEDULE OF MASSES

Sunday: 9:00 a.m., 11:00 a.m.
Monday–Friday: 7:00 a.m.
Spanish: 2:00 p.m. Last Saturday of every month
Holy Days of Obligation: noon

ACTIVITIES

Novenas in English and Spanish: Second Sunday of the month, 3:00 p.m.
Bible Class
Adult and Teen Retreats
Days of Recollection
Lecture and Video on the Life of Mother Cabrini
Birthday Party for Mother Cabrini in July
Special Children's Programs

Holy Infant Jesus Shrine

DIOCESE OF BUFFALO
3452 NIAGARA FALLS BOULEVARD • NORTH TONAWANDA, NY 14120 • (716) 694-4313

HISTORY OF THE SHRINE

The Holy Infant Jesus Shrine at Wheatfield, N.Y., was dedicated January 20, 1979, by the Most Rev. Edward D. Head, bishop of Buffalo. Transformed from a one-room country school built in 1887, the new shrine replaced the old shrine, which was dedicated by the Most Rev. Aloysius Burke on April 30, 1958.

The Infant Jesus statue, venerated in the shrine, is a replica of the renowned original statue revered at San Salvatore in Onda Church, in Rome, since the times of St. Vincent Pallotti. This statue symbolizes the immense mercy of God.

The Holy Infant Jesus Shrine is not a parish church. It is a house of prayer and worship, where everyone is free to come, individually or as members of a group or a pilgrimage, to pray and to celebrate the mysteries of our religion, initiated with the Incarnation of the Son of God.

The specific purpose of the shrine apostolate is the deepening of the awareness that we are adopted sons and daughters of God, extending the image and spirit of Christ in the world.

SCHEDULE OF MASSES
Sunday: 11:00 a.m.
Daily: 6:45 a.m.
Thursday: 7:00 p.m.
Holy Day of Obligation: 6:45 a.m.
Confessions: Upon request

DEVOTIONS
Mass, Novena to the Infant Jesus, Exposition of the Blessed Sacrament with
    the Holy Rosary: Thursday, 7:00 p.m.
All-Night Vigils: Thursday–Friday, monthly March–November

FACILITIES
Counseling Center

LANGUAGES
English, Polish, Italian, and German

Shrine of
Our Lady of the Island

DIOCESE OF ROCKVILLE CENTRE
EASTPORT MANOR ROAD • P.O. BOX 26 • ROCKVILLE CENTRE, NY 11941 • (516) 325-0661

HISTORY OF THE SHRINE

In 1953, seventy acres in Eastport, Long Island, were donated to the Montfort Missionaries by Mr. Crescenzo Vigliotta Sr., for a shrine to honor Mary, Mother of God. In 1957, surrounding acres overlooking Moriches Bay were given to the Missionaries. The shrine officially opened in 1975 with the unveiling of the 25-ton statue of Mary placed on an 18-foot pedestal of rocks facing the Atlantic Ocean. The Blessed Sacrament Chapel was constructed in 1976, followed by the dedication of the shrine in October of that year. Since then, outdoor Stations of the Cross, the rosary walk, pilgrim hall, office building and gift shop, pro-life shrine, Pieta, and Shrine to St. Joseph have been added.

In May 1990, the International Rosary Day was observed at the shrine by a special Rosary Procession, Holy Sacrifice of the Mass, Exposition of the Blessed Sacrament, and Perpetual Rosary. Annually, on August 15, an outdoor Mass is celebrated at noon followed by a conferral of the Sacrament of the Sick. The sacrament is intended for those afflicted with serious illnesses as well as those who are sixty years of age or older. The shrine has been directed by the Montfort Missionaries since 1972.

SCHEDULE OF MASSES
Sunday: 10:00 a.m.
Daily: 9:30 a.m.
Holy Day of Obligation: 10:00 a.m.
Confessions: Upon request

DEVOTIONS
Rosary: Sunday, 3:00 p.m.
Immaculate Conception: December 8, 10:00 a.m.
Blessing of Bikes (Blue Knights): Last Sunday in April
Divine Mercy Mass: First Wednesdays, noon

FACILITIES

Outdoor Stations of the Cross and Rosary Walk
Pilgrim Hall (accommodates 300)
Gift Shop
Coffee Shop

Holy Dormition (Assumption) Grotto

UKRAINIAN CATHOLIC DIOCESE OF STAMFORD
ST. MARY'S VILLA, (SPIRITUAL AND EDUCATIONAL CENTER),
P.O. BOX 6, 150 SISTERS SERVANTS LANE, SLOATSBURG, NY 10974-9617
(914) 753-5100

HISTORY OF THE SHRINE

The Sisters Servants of Mary Immaculate, a congregation of sisters in the Ukrainian Byzantine tradition, operate and maintain an indoor/outdoor shrine to Our Lady—The Holy Dormition (Assumption).

Visitors are always welcome to the outdoor shrine. The annual pilgrimage takes place on the weekend before the Feast of the Dormition (Assumption) of Our Lady with a candlelight procession and service on Saturday evening. Services are in English and Ukrainian.

The indoor shrine welcomes visitors throughout the year for private visits or to join the community in its prayers. The chapel has an icon of the Holy Dormition. The indoor shrine is located within the retreat house setting. It is requested that groups planning to visit the shrine call prior to arrival.

There are no regularly scheduled public Masses at the shrine.

Marian Shrine—
National Shrine of Mary
Help of Christians

ARCHDIOCESE OF NEW YORK
FILORS LANE • WEST HAVERSTRAW, NY 10993 • (914) 947-2200

HISTORY OF THE SHRINE

The Salesians of Don Bosco built a rosary way here in 1954 in observance of the Marian Year. Fifteen life-size marble statues were placed along a wooded path. People came in increasing numbers to pray along this gospel trail. As the number of pilgrims grew, the shrine was formally established.

Over the years, additional items were added to beautify the Marian shrine. These include the 48-foot bronze Rosary Madonna statue; the majestic altar of Mary that serves as an outdoor cathedral; a glass-enclosed pavilion chapel; grottoes depicting the apparitions at Fatima and Lourdes; the Becchi House (a replica of the home where St. John Bosco grew up); the large, marble Stations of the Cross; and a memorial to The Unborn.

The shrine is a place for spiritual renewal through pilgrimages, retreats, and days of study and recollection. The Salesians strive to make the shrine a place where all can encounter the Lord with the help of Mary. The Blessed Sacrament Chapel is open for prayer and meditation Sundays from 9:00 a.m. to 5:00 p.m.

Among the large groups that hold their celebrations at the shrine are the Salesian Family, the Cursillistas, the Charismatics, Pro-Life, Jornadas de Vida Cristiana, Pascua Juvenil, Marian Movement of Priests, and Friends of Maria Goretti. Some of the feasts celebrated here are Divine Mercy Sunday, Feast of Mary Help of Christians, Our Lady of Mount Carmel, the Assumption, and Saint John Bosco. Family days are enjoyed by Polish, Italian, Latino, Filipino, Korean, and Vietnamese organizations.

SCHEDULE OF MASSES

Sunday: May–October, 11:00 a.m.,12:30 p.m.; November–April, noon
Daily: noon
Holy Days of Obligation: noon
Confessions: Before Mass and upon request

DEVOTIONS
Rosary Procession (when requested by group)
Rosary (after daily Mass)
Eucharistic Adoration: Wednesday, 8:00 p.m.
Stations of the Cross
Processions: Feast of Mary Help of Christians (May 24); Feast of the Assumption (August 15)
Retreats: By reservation only
Days of Recollection: By reservation only
Marriage Preparation: Monthly, by special arrangement

NOVENAS
St. John Bosco, January 22–30
Mary Help of Christians, May 15–23
Immaculate Conception, November 29–December 7

PREPARATION FOR THE MILLENNIUM
Prayer and Study Days
Retreats
Conferences

FACILITIES
Adult Retreat Center
Youth Retreat Center
Renewal Center (ample space for workshops)
Overnight Accommodations
Religious Bookstore
Gift Shop

LANGUAGES
English, Spanish, Italian, French, and Polish

Our Lady of Fatima Shrine

DIOCESE OF BUFFALO

1023 SWANN ROAD • YOUNGSTOWN, NY 14174-0167 • (716) 754-7489

HISTORY OF THE SHRINE

Through the interaction between the Barnabite Fathers, newly arrived from Italy in 1954, and the people of western New York, this shrine was created and dedicated to the 1917 miracle at Fatima, Portugal, where the Blessed Virgin appeared to three shepherds and asked for prayer and sacrifice so that "Our Lord may save humanity from all calamities and bring peace to the world. . . ." She encouraged a simple daily formula for prayer—the rosary—and the need to live the Gospel.

In 1962, the Basilica of Our Lady of the Rosary, built in the shape of a globe with a large statue of the Blessed Virgin Mary standing atop it—symbolizing her prayers for the entire world—became the center of the shrine complex, which includes other chapels and facilities. The large statue of Our Lady, sculpted from Vermont granite, is more than 13-feet high and weighs ten tons. Within the basilica, behind the altar, is the *Peace Mural* that was created by Polish artist Joseph Slawinski in 1975. Within the basilica are two smaller chapels: the Blessed Sacrament Chapel and the Immaculate Heart Chapel. Outside, in front of the basilica is a giant rosary circling a heart-shaped pond, and the Avenue of the Saints, lined by more than one hundred life-size statues of holy women and men declared Saints of the Church. Also on the grounds are a replica of the first little chapel built at Fatima, Portugal, and the original chapel built here (now englobed in the shrine auxiliary building).

Special events in the year at the shrine are the Coronation of the Blessed Mother on the second Sunday in August and the Festival of Lights through the month of December.

SCHEDULE OF MASSES

Sunday Vigil: 4:00 p.m.
Sunday: 9:00 a.m., noon, 5:00 p.m.
Daily: 11:30 a.m., 4:00 p.m.
Holy Day of Obligation: 9:00 a.m., noon, 5:00 p.m.
Thanksgiving: 11:30 a.m.
Christmas: 12:00 a.m., 9:00 a.m., noon
Easter: midnight, 9:00 a.m., noon, 5:00 p.m.
Reconciliation: Fifteen minutes before liturgies

DEVOTIONS

Novenas: Lent, All Souls' Day, Mother's Day, Father's Day
Rosary and Benediction: Sunday, 3:00 p.m.
Adoration of the Blessed Sacrament: Daily

FACILITIES

Gift Shop
Cafeteria

LANGUAGES

English, French, Spanish, Italian, and Portuguese

National Shrine Centre—
Our Lady of Guadalupe,
Mother of the Americas

DIOCESE OF ALLENTOWN
501 RIDGE AVENUE • ALLENTOWN, PA 18102 • (610) 433-4404

HISTORY OF THE SHRINE

St. John Neumann founded the first Catholic parish in Allentown, Pa., which he called the Church of the Immaculate Conception of the Blessed Virgin Mary. It was built by Irish immigrants who came here seeking religious freedom.

The church is now the National Shrine Centre and has a steeple that stands 185-feet high. It has some of the finest examples of painted and stained-glass windows made in Germany; sixteen beautiful windows depict the life of the Blessed Virgin Mary. The last window is that of the Sacred Heart of Jesus. On the ceiling are three huge canvasses: The Annunciation, The Immaculate Conception, and The Coronation.

The shrine is on the side altar where the pilgrims can get a close-up view of what is considered the finest reproduction of the Guadalupe picture. It is said "Go to Allentown; if you can't, go to Mexico."

The shrine was dedicated on Saturday, October 5, 1974, by Bishop Joseph McShea, the first bishop of Allentown; Bishop Sidney L. Metzger of El Paso, Texas; Bishop John Venancio of Fatima, Portugal; archabbot of the Basilica of Guadalupe, Guilliamo Schulmberg, and the archpriest of the Basilica of Guadalupe, both of Mexico City.

SCHEDULE OF MASSES
Sunday Vigil: 4:15 p.m.
Sundays: 8:00 a.m., 10:30 a.m., noon
Daily: 6:30 a.m., 8:00 a.m.
First Friday: 6:30 a.m., 8:00 a.m.
Holy Day of Obligation Vigil: 6:45 p.m.
Holy Day of Obligation: 8:00 a.m., 6:45 p.m.

DEVOTIONS
Novena in Honor of Our Lady of Guadalupe: Monday, 8:00 a.m.
Rosary: 7:45 a.m.

Blessed Katharine Drexel Shrine

MOTHERHOUSE OF THE SISTERS OF THE BLESSED SACRAMENT
ARCHDIOCESE OF PHILADELPHIA
1663 BRISTOL PIKE • BENSALEM, PA 19020-8502 • (215) 244-9900, EXT. 22

HISTORY OF THE SHRINE

A woman of the nineteenth and twentieth centuries, Katharine Drexel of Philadelphia was pronounced Blessed by Pope John Paul II in November 1988.

Katharine Drexel was a wealthy socialite who became a woman religious. She began a congregation called the Sisters of the Blessed Sacrament in 1891. Mother Katharine chose as her life's mission to serve the poor among the African Americans and Native Americans of her day. She died in 1955 at age 96 and is buried at the Blessed Katharine Drexel Shrine.

Blessed Katharine Drexel's intense devotion to the Holy Eucharist is the driving spiritual force in her congregation's work today.

SCHEDULE OF MASSES
Call for information.

DEVOTIONS
Blessed Sacrament on exposition daily, except in Summer.

FACILITIES
Open daily, 1:00–5:00 p.m.
Shrine Shop and Gift Shop
Extended group pilgrimages (call for reservations).
Guild Newsletter (call to order).

National Shrine of Our Lady of Czestochowa

ARCHDIOCESE OF PHILADELPHIA

P.O. BOX 2049 • FERRY ROAD • DOYLESTOWN, PA 18901 • (215) 345-0600

HISTORY OF THE SHRINE

The National Shrine of Our Lady of Czestochowa, built as a center of Marian devotion, was dedicated on October 16, 1966, in commemoration of the celebration of one thousand years of Poland's Christianity (966). It stands atop Beacon Hill in Bucks County. The original barn chapel, used as the main place of worship until the shrine's completion, stands on the shrine property as a testament of the shrine's humble beginnings.

The shrine is open throughout the year as a spiritual and cultural center for Americans of Polish descent, and for all visitors wishing to come in pilgrimage. There are pilgrimages of Spanish, Haitian, French, and Italian apostolates.

The main religious celebration of the year is the Feast of Our Lady of Czestochowa. On average, 6,000 people attend this celebration. Approximately 500,000 people visit the shrine annually.

SCHEDULE OF MASSES

Sunday Vigil: 5:00 p.m.
Sunday: 8:00 a.m., 9:00 a.m., 10:00 a.m., 11:00 a.m., noon, 2:00 p.m., 5:00 p.m.
Holy Day of Obligation Vigil: 5:00 p.m.
Holy Day of Obligation: 7:30 a.m., 8:00 a.m., 11:30 a.m., 5:00 p.m., 7:00 p.m.
Confessions: Daily before 11:30 a.m. Mass; Sunday, 8:00 a.m.–5:30 p.m.

DEVOTIONS

Novenas: Weekly
Rosary: Daily
Holy Hour: First Friday and First Saturday
Devotion in preparation for the Year 2000: All-Night Vigil, last Saturday of the month
9:00 p.m. Saturday to 5:00 a.m. Sunday

FACILITIES
Religious Bookstore
Gift Shop
Cafeteria

CEMETERY
Polish Veterans section, Honor section for Polish people of prominence, Clergy
section, and section for Americans of Polish descent

LANGUAGES
English, Polish, Spanish, and French

Grotto of Our Lady of Lourdes— Sisters of St. Basil the Great

METROPOLITAN ARCHDIOCESE OF PHILADELPHIA, UKRAINIAN
710 FOX CHASE ROAD • FOX CHASE MANOR, PA 19046-4198
(215) 663-9153 • (215) 342-4222 • FAX (215) 728-6129

HISTORY OF THE SHRINE

The first pilgrimage to the Grotto of Our Lady of Lourdes on the grounds of the Sisters of St. Basil the Great was inaugurated by the Very Reverend Mother M. Josaphat Teodorowych, OSBM, major superior, on Mother's Day, 1938.

A plenary indulgence was granted in 1940 by the Holy See to all faithful who participated in the pilgrimage. Annually, pilgrims primarily from the Ukrainian Catholic parishes attend. All are welcome! The Pilgrimage is held on Mother's Day.

SCHEDULE OF MASSES
Call for Mass schedule

FACILITIES
Basilian Gift Shop
Ukrainian Cultural Center

LANGUAGES
English and Ukrainian

Year 2000: Dedication of a Basilian Chapel Spirituality Center

Basilica of
The Sacred Heart of Jesus

DIOCESE OF HARRISBURG
30 BASILICA DRIVE • HANOVER, PA 17331-8924 • (717) 637-2721

HISTORY OF THE SHRINE

The Basilica of the Sacred Heart of Jesus, named a basilica by Pope John XXIII on June 30, 1962, was called the Conewago Chapel in colonial times. The chapel was built in 1741 by Fr. William Wappeler, SJ, a priest sent to minister to the German Catholic immigrants in the area. The chapel was dedicated to St. Mary of the Assumption, but immediately was known as Conewago Chapel.

By 1784, the congregation had grown to more than a thousand members, and a new church was constructed and completed in 1787. Fr. Pellentz named this imposing edifice Sacred Heart of Jesus. It became the first parish church in America dedicated to the loving heart of our Divine Savior, and it is the oldest Catholic church building made of stone in the country.

In 1800, the church property was renamed the Conewago Plantation, as it had gradually grown from a Mass station and log chapel to the largest parish in the United States. In 1850, the building was again enlarged by the addition of a transept and apse, under the direction of Fr. Joseph Enders, SJ. Fr. Enders also enlarged the small oratory near the vestibule to serve as a daily chapel. A beautiful painting of the Assumption of Mary was received in 1987, and the chapel was renovated and renamed as Our Lady's Chapel that same year. The church was turned over to the Diocese of Harrisburg on June 3, 1901.

SCHEDULE OF MASSES

Sunday Vigil: 6:30 p.m.
Sunday: 7:30 a.m., 10:00 a.m.
Weekday: 7:00 a.m. (school days); 8:00 a.m. (other weekdays)
Holy Day of Obligation Vigil: 7:00 p.m.
Holy Day of Obligation: 5:30 a.m., 11:00 a.m., 7:00 p.m.
Confessions: Saturday, 4:00 p.m., 6:00 p.m.; Sunday, 9:30 a.m.

DEVOTIONS
First Friday: 11:00 a.m. (during school year), 7:00 p.m.

FACILITIES
Bus Tours (arranged in advance)

Shrine of the Sacred Heart

DIOCESE OF SCRANTON
BOX 500 • HARLEIGH, PA 18225 • (717) 455-1162

HISTORY OF THE SHRINE

 Situated in the Harleigh section of Hazleton, in the Diocese of Scranton, is the largest outdoor shrine in North America devoted to the Sacred Heart. It is a contemporary reminder of the majesty of the Sacred Heart and a serene embodiment of devotion to him.

The shrine depicts the life of Christ, beginning with the Nativity scene. The shrine is constructed on a slight incline with five plateaus, each containing a multicolored geometric walk along which are plaques depicting the Twelve Promises of the Sacred Heart to St. Margaret Mary Alocoque. A winding pathway contains the Stations of the Cross, each made of Carrara marble set on green granite slabs. The focal point of the shrine is the statue of the Sacred Heart, also of Carrara marble, with a huge crown over the whole setting. A large crucifixion scene with the tomb of the Unborn Child stands in its own beauty as a reminder of the abortion plague confronting our society today. A replica of the tomb of Christ embedded in the mountainside completes the attractions.

The shrine, founded by Fr. Girard F. Angelo in 1975, has been the scene of the National Congress of the Sacred Heart and many other conferences throughout the years. It serves as the National Headquarters for the Men of the Sacred Heart and serves as the Diocesan Office for Apostleship of Prayer (League of the Sacred Heart).

The shrine is open throughout the year. Individuals and groups are welcome.

SCHEDULE OF MASSES
Sunday Vigil: 6:00 p.m.
Sunday: 8:00 a.m., 10:00 a.m.
Holy Day of Obligation Vigil: 7:00 p.m.
Holy Day of Obligation: 8:00 a.m., 7:00 p.m.

DEVOTIONS
Novenas: Monthly
Rosary: Weekly

FACILITIES
Religious Gift Shop
Overnight Accommodations
Cafeteria
Cultural Center

LANGUAGES
English, Italian, and Spanish

SPECIAL PROGRAMS
Preparation for the celebration of the Third Millennium

National Shrine of St. John Neumann

ARCHDIOCESE OF PHILADELPHIA
ST. PETER THE APOSTLE CHURCH • 5TH STREET AND GIRARD AVENUE
PHILADELPHIA, PA 19123 • (215) 627-3080

HISTORY OF THE SHRINE

St. John Neumann, one of the pioneers of the Catholic Church in the United States, was responsible for organizing the diocesan schedule of the Forty Hours Devotion, the establishment of the first system of parochial schools and the first church in America for Italians, and the founding of the Glen Riddle group of the Third Order of the Sisters of St. Francis.

Neumann was born in 1811, in Bohemia, and left his native land to be a missionary in America. In 1836, he was ordained by Bishop John Dubois in New York. Neumann joined the Redemptorists four years later, and was the first to make his religious profession as a Redemptorist in the New World. A decade later he was consecrated fourth bishop of Philadelphia by order of Pope Pius IX.

At forty-eight years of age, exhausted from his endeavors, he died on the street a few blocks from Logan Square, the site of his new cathedral. His remains now repose in the crypt of St. Peter's Church in Philadelphia. Pope Benedict XV said of his remarkable life, "You are all bound to imitate Venerable Neumann." The Vatican Congregation for the Causes of Saints has officially verified that three people are alive today because of the intercession of Bishop Neumann. The miracle in 1963 paved the way for his canonization by Pope Paul VI on June 19, 1977.

The shrine is open daily from 7:30 a.m. to 6:00 p.m. and Sunday from 7:30 a.m. to 5:00 p.m. Pilgrimage groups are welcome.

SCHEDULE OF MASSES

Sunday Vigil: 5:30 p.m.
Sunday: 7:30 a.m., 9:30 a.m., 11:00 a.m. (Spanish), 12:30 p.m., 3:30 p.m.
Weekday: 7:30 a.m., 12:15 p.m., 5:30 p.m.

DEVOTIONS

St. John Neumann Novena: Weekday, after 12:15 p.m. Mass, except Wednesday; Sunday, after 3:30 p.m. Mass

Our Lady of Perpetual Help Novena: Wednesday, after 12:15 p.m. Mass

First Friday: Exposition 1:00–6:00 p.m.

First Saturday: 10:00 a.m. (nuns' holy hour and Mass); 12:15 p.m. (Mass and Fatima vigil until 2:45 p.m.)

FACILITIES

Shrine Museum and Exhibit

Gift Shop

National Shrine of St. Rita of Cascia

ARCHDIOCESE OF PHILADELPHIA
1166 SOUTH BROAD STREET • PHILADELPHIA, PA 19146
(215) 546-8333 • FAX (215) 732-3510

HISTORY OF THE SHRINE

Wife and mother, widow and Augustinian nun, Saint of the Impossible and Advocate of Difficult Cases, Reconciler and Promoter of Family Harmony: these are some of the titles by which St. Rita is known and venerated around the world. Married at 16 and widowed by an assassin's knife at 32, her Christian faith led Rita to forgive her husband's murderer and to implore her sons to do the same. At their death soon after, she entered the convent of the Augustinian nuns in Cascia, Italy. For the last 15 years of her life she bore the stigmata in the unique form of a thorn on her forehead.

It was in 1907 that the Augustinian Friars from Villanova, Penn. established the Church of St. Rita in Philadelphia, to serve the growing Italian immigrant population of this city. St. Rita had been canonized only seven years previously and devotion to her was extremely popular. The friars immediately initiated a weekly novena, which drew faithful from near and far to seek the intercession of this blessed woman whose reputation as "Saint of the Impossible" was spreading quickly. The original basement church became the center of devotion to St. Rita throughout the country, and within several years the majestic upper church, designed in the style of fourteenth-century Renaissance architecture, was completed. The stained-glass windows and paintings adorning the church depict scenes from the lives of St. Rita, St. Augustine, and other figures of Augustinian history and spirituality. Preserved in the church are precious relics of St. Rita and of Blessed Stephen Bellesini, nineteenth-century Augustinian patron of youth and of the sick.

SCHEDULE OF MASSES

Sunday Vigil: 5:00 p.m.
Sunday: 9:00 a.m., 11:00 a.m.
Weekdays: 8:00 a.m., noon; also Wednesdays, 7:30 p.m.
Saturday: 8:00 a.m.
Confessions: Monday–Saturday

DEVOTIONS
St. Rita Perpetual Novena: Every Wednesday following the three Masses
Feast of Blessed Stephen Bellesini: February 3
St. Rita Solemn Novena: May 13–May 21
St. Rita Solemn Feast: May 22, with blessing of roses
Triduum to Sts. Monica and Augustine: August 26, 27, 28

FACILITIES
Gift Shop
St. Rita Newsletter available upon request.

Shrine of Our Lady of the Miraculous Medal

ARCHDIOCESE OF PHILADELPHIA
CENTRAL ASSOCIATION OF THE MIRACULOUS MEDAL
475 E. CHELTEN AVENUE • PHILADELPHIA, PA 19144 • (800) 523-3674

HISTORY OF THE SHRINE

Mary's Central Shrine was built in gratitude to Mary by the Promoters and Members of the Central Association of the Miraculous Medal. This Pious Association, established in Philadelphia in 1915, has as its primary purpose the spread of devotion to Mary Immaculate through the Miraculous Medal. Toward this end, the association has distributed more than 75 million Miraculous Medals and 40 million booklets telling the story of the Medal and containing the Medal Novena prayers.

The Perpetual Novena, begun here in 1930, has added considerable fame to Mary's Central Shrine. It started with one service each Monday, but soon mushroomed until, now, nine novena services every Monday of the year gather the heartfelt petitions of more than two thousand devotees of Mary and speed them heavenward to her. From this shrine, the Perpetual Novena has spread to thousands of parishes in the United States and abroad.

The Miraculous Medal, which gives its name to this shrine, is unique in that it is the only medal designed by Mary herself, during her apparitions to St. Catherine Labouré. Above the gorgeous shrine altar, as its centerpiece, stands a life-size white marble statue of Mary as she appeared to St. Catherine and asked that a medal be made after that model. This statue is truly one of the most exquisite and appealing of Our Lady in modern art.

Unlike Lourdes and other famous shrines, here no stacks of crutches or braces or canes are left after miraculous cures. Instead, historically, miracles of graces are worked in the secrecy of the Marian shrine's confessional, which is occupied by confessors from early morning to late night every Monday during all the novena services.

SCHEDULE OF MASSES

Sundays and Holy Days: 9:00 a.m.
Daily: 8:00 a.m., 12:05 p.m. (except Monday)
Mondays: 7:00 a.m., 9:00 a.m., 12:05 p.m.

DEVOTIONS

Miraculous Medal Novena: 7:00 a.m., 9:00 a.m. (at Mass), 2:00 p.m., 3:00 p.m.,
    4:00 p.m., 5:00 p.m., 6:00 p.m., 7:00 p.m., 8:00 p.m.
Solemn Novena: Nine successive days preceding the Feast of Our Lady of the
    Miraculous Medal, November 27

SHRINE HOURS

11:00 a.m.–4:00 p.m. Sunday–Saturday (except Monday)
All day Monday

St. Anthony's Chapel
Shrine of Many Relics

DIOCESE OF PITTSBURGH
MOST HOLY NAME CHURCH
1704 HARPSTER STREET • PITTSBURGH, PA 15212 • (412) 323-9504

HISTORY OF THE SHRINE

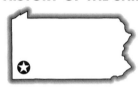

Construction began on the chapel in 1880 under the direction of Fr. Suitbert G. Mollinger, who was the son of a wealthy Belgian family and the first pastor of Most Holy Name of Jesus Church. Fr. Mollinger personally financed the building of the devotional chapel to house his large collection of relics. Dedication of the chapel took place on the Feast of St. Anthony, June 13, 1883. Thousands of people made their way to visit the shrine and to be blessed by Fr. Mollinger and the relic of St. Anthony, the most venerated of all relics in the chapel.

Since then, more than 4,000 relics of the saints and blesseds have reposed peacefully in more than 800 ornate cases in the chapel. Among these relics are reminders of the most profound aspects of the faith: splinters of the True Cross and of the Last Supper table, pieces of instruments from the scourging of Jesus, and other elements from the Passion.

The Chapel of St. Anthony of Padua has been sanctified by the prayers of the faithful for more than a century. It is hoped that visits to the chapel and prayers through the intercession of The Wonder Worker will enable the good works of St. Anthony to bless the faithful for many years. The chapel is located next to the rectory of Most Holy Name Church and is administered by the parish.

The chapel is open Sundays, 11:00 a.m.– 4:00 p.m. (tour guide available); and Tuesdays, Thursdays, and Saturdays, 1:00–4:00 p.m. It is closed on holidays. Call St. Anthony's Chapel to arrange group tours or to purchase a video on the chapel's history.

SCHEDULE OF MASSES

Sunday Vigil: 6:00 p.m. (Most Holy Name Church)
Sunday: 7:30 a.m., 9:00 a.m., 11:30 a.m. (Most Holy Name Church)
Daily: 8:30 a.m. (Most Holy Name Church)
Tuesday: 8:30 a.m. with St. Anthony Novena (St. Anthony's Chapel)

DEVOTIONS
Novena to St. Anthony: Tuesday, after 8:30 a.m. Mass
Novena to St. Anthony and Benediction: Tuesday, 7:30 p.m.

FACILITIES
Gift Shop
Museum
Accessible to people with disabilities

Basilica of the National Shrine of St. Ann

DIOCESE OF SCRANTON
PASSIONIST FATHERS AND BROTHERS • SCRANTON, PA 18504-3098 • (717) 347-5691

HISTORY OF THE SHRINE

The Passionist Fathers concluded negotiations for the establishment of a monastery in Scranton on September 8, 1902. Within a few weeks, the new foundation was placed under the patronage of St. Ann. The monastery was dedicated on July 2, 1905. On July 17 of that year, according to Passionist custom, the community began a novena in honor of St. Ann. The devotions were held within the monastic enclosure. The novena was repeated each year in the chapel attended only by members of the community.

In 1924, at the request of the laity, novena devotions were held in the small public chapel. The crowds increased so rapidly that, within a month, additional services had to be provided. Even then the chapel was not large enough to accommodate the crowds, so a huge tent was erected on the monastery grounds. Next came a larger wooden structure. This, too, was only temporary. Finally, the magnificent structure that is now St. Ann's Monastery National Shrine was dedicated on April 2, 1929. By an Apostolic Bull dated August 29, 1996, Pope John Paul II raised St. Ann's to the status of basilica.

Weekly novena devotions are conducted each Monday of the year.

During the Solemn Novena in honor of St. Ann, conducted each year from July 17 to the Feast Day of St. Ann on July 26, there is a beautiful and inspiring manifestation of faith and devotion at St. Ann's Shrine. Thousands come from far and near to visit and pray at the shrine. This is the history of the Passionist devotion to St. Ann which continues to be spread throughout the whole world.

DEVOTIONS

Novena to St. Ann: Every Monday, 8:00 a.m., noon, 3:30 p.m., 5:30 p.m., 7:30 p.m. Confessions after each devotion.

Solemn Novena to St. Ann: July 17–26: 8:00 a.m., 11:45 a.m., 3:30 p.m., 5:30 p.m., 7:30 p.m. Confessions are held before and after each devotion.

On the Feast of St. Ann, July 26, confessions begin at 4:00 a.m. and continue throughout the day. The first Mass of the day is at 4:30 a.m. Masses and Novena devotions continue throughout the day to the final closing at 7:30 p.m.

Shrine of Our Lady of Perpetual Help

METROPOLITAN ARCHDIOCESE OF PITTSBURGH, BYZANTINE
510 WEST MAIN STREET • BOX 878 • UNIONTOWN, PA 15401 • (412) 438-7149

HISTORY OF THE SHRINE

In 1935, Pope Pius XI presented the Sisters of the Order of St. Basil the Great with an icon of Our Lady of Perpetual Help. This icon is a reproduction of the miraculous icon that is venerated in the Church of St. Alphonsus in Rome. In entrusting this icon to the sisters, Pope Pius XI requested that devotion to the Mother of God, under the title of Our Lady of Perpetual Help, be promoted.

The Shrine of Our Lady of Perpetual Help is in Mount St. Macrina Retreat Center, a mansion built in 1902. The shrine is staffed by the Sisters of the Order of St. Basil the Great, a Byzantine Rite community.

Individuals and groups are invited to make day pilgrimages to the shrine. Contact the Director of the Retreat Center to make arrangements.

Each Labor Day Weekend, a pilgrimage for thousands of Byzantine and Roman Rite Catholics is held on the grounds of Mount St. Macrina in honor of Our Lady of Perpetual Help.

SCHEDULE OF MASSES

There are no regularly scheduled Masses, although there are private liturgies for retreat groups.

DEVOTIONS

The Retreat Center offers various types of retreats, workshops, and days of reflection. The Center is also available for anyone seeking quiet and solitude as a respite from their busy schedules, whether for a day or longer. Day pilgrimages to the shrine are also encouraged.

FACILITIES

There are more than one hundred acres of natural beauty, dotted with outdoor shrines and chapels for private prayer. The Retreat Center is an elegant mansion with conference rooms, a chapel, and a dining area that seats forty-five people. There are overnight accommodations for thirty people in small dormitory-style rooms. In a nearby annex, there are six semi-private rooms. There is also a Religious Gift Shop and an Icon Shop.

LANGUAGES

English and Slavonic

The Shrine of the Little Flower

DIOCESE OF PROVIDENCE
7 DION DRIVE, NASONVILLE • HARRISVILLE, RI 02830 • (401) 568-8280
INTERNET: HTTP://USERS.IDS.NET/~STF/S/ • E-MAIL: STF@IDS.NET

HISTORY OF THE SHRINE

It is believed that a parishioner was cured through the intercession of St. Theresa of the Child Jesus in 1923. This is the first shrine in the United States dedicated to St. Theresa. Although small in size, the shrine attracts thousands of people from the New England area, yet it remains a place of refuge and prayer nestled under tall trees on the grounds.

The Feast of St. Theresa of the Child Jesus is celebrated in the shrine on the Sunday closest to October 1.

SCHEDULE OF MASSES
Sunday Vigil: 5:00 p.m.
Sunday: 8:00 a.m., 10:30 a.m.
Daily: 8:30 a.m.
Holy Day of Obligation Vigil: 7:00 p.m.
Holy Day of Obligation: 8:30 a.m., 7:00 p.m.
Confessions: Saturday, 4:00 p.m.

DEVOTIONS
Rosary: Tuesday, 6:30 p.m.
Annual Feast Day Celebration: Third Sunday in August, including outdoor rosary, solemn Mass procession, food, and religious gift booth.

FACILITIES
Outdoor Stations of the Cross
Scala Sancta (Holy Stairs)
Living Rosary
Grotto with outdoor altar for Masses (seating cap. about 500)
Plenty of parking and accessible to the disabled
Parish church for indoor prayer before the Blessed Sacrament

LANGUAGES
English and French

St. Anne's Shrine

DIOCESE OF BURLINGTON
ISLE LA MOTTE, VT 05463 • (802) 928-3362

HISTORY OF THE SHRINE

 St. Anne's Shrine nestles close by beautiful Lake Champlain on Isle La Motte. The shrine is situated on the site of Fort St. Anne, Vermont's oldest settlement, constructed in 1666, where the first Mass in Vermont was celebrated. Though the fort itself was short-lived, the site continued to be a favorite stopping place for Lake Champlain travelers in the succeeding years of war and peace.

The shrine is run by the Edmundite Fathers and Brothers and is open May 15–October 15. Eucharistic celebrations are held daily in the open-air pavilion.

SCHEDULE OF MASSES

Sunday Vigil: 7:00 p.m.
Sunday: 8:30 a.m., 10:00 a.m., 11:15 a.m., 4:00 p.m.
Monday–Friday: 11:15 a.m.; Rosary, 11:00 a.m.
Holy Day of Obligation Vigil: 7:00 p.m.
Holy Day of Obligation: 8:30 a.m., 10:00 a.m., 11:15 a.m., 4:00 p.m.
Confessions: Before all Masses and Devotions

DEVOTIONS

Rosary: Monday–Friday, 11:00 a.m.
Novenas: Triduums in honor of St. Anne, July 23–26; in honor of Blessed Mother,
    August 13–15

FACILITIES

Gift Shop
Cafeteria
All-Purpose Building
Stations of the Cross
Grottos
Beach/Dock
Picnic Grounds

LANGUAGES

English and French

South

Shrine of the Blessed Sacrament

DIOCESE OF BIRMINGHAM
OUR LADY OF THE ANGELS MONASTERY
5817 OLD LEEDS ROAD • BIRMINGHAM, AL 35210 • (205) 956-9537 • FAX (205) 956-0328
INTERNET: HTTP://WWW.EWTN.COM

HISTORY OF THE SHRINE

Mother M. Angelica founded Our Lady of the Angels Monastery, of Poor Clare Nuns of Perpetual Adoration, in 1962. She was a founding member of Sancta Clara Monastery in Canton, Ohio, where she fell and injured her spine. Doctors told her she had only a 50-percent chance of walking again. In a moment of panic, she promised the Lord she would build a Monastery of Perpetual Adoration in the South, if she were permitted to walk again. She arrived in Birmingham in February 1961; the monastery was built and dedicated by May 20, 1962.

In 1980, Mother Angelica built a television studio behind the monastery to aid the diocese, bishops, and priests in producing Catholic television programs. The Eternal Word Television Network (EWTN) began transmitting programs via satellite to cable systems across the United States on August 15, 1981. EWTN is devoted to proclaiming the power of the Gospel, the depth of God's love, and the wonder of God's presence. On September 1, 1987, EWTN began broadcasting 24 hours a day; it carried live coverage of the Holy Father's visit to the United States.

In the summer of 1991, the chapel of Our Lady of the Angels Monastery was declared the Shrine of the Blessed Sacrament by Bishop Raymond Boland. This aids the monastery in promoting eucharistic tours and adoration among the faithful. Over the years, numerous pilgrims have descended upon the Shrine of the Blessed Sacrament to experience a time of renewal and reflection.

The Shrine of the Blessed Sacrament, located on the grounds of Our Lady of the Angels Monastery, allows pilgrims the opportunity to "come away by yourself to a quiet place, and rest a while" (Mk 6:31). The shrine allows individuals to adore our Lord, who is exposed perpetually in the Blessed Sacrament. The grounds of the shrine are full of reminders of God's beauty. The Stations of the Cross, Shrine of the Unborn, and Pieta, are available for personal meditation. Two outdoor altars are used for special feast day celebrations.

Retreats are arranged for groups of ten or more. Individual pilgrims may join any group on retreat or make a private retreat. This unforgettable experience evolves around a schedule of Mass, rosary, confession, healing service, spiritual talks, and guided tours. The shrine has coordinated special group rates with local hotels. Box lunches can be arranged upon request. The Shrine of the Blessed Sacrament is open to people of all faiths. Modest attire is requested.

SCHEDULE OF MASSES

Sunday: 7:00 a.m., noon
Daily: 7:00 a.m., noon
Holy Day of Obligation: 7:00 a.m., noon
Confession: Daily, 11:00 a.m.–noon and by appointment

DEVOTIONS

Healing Service: Sunday 5:00 p.m.
Holy Hour: Thursday, 7:00 p.m.
Rosary

FACILITIES

Two Outdoor Altars
Stations of the Cross
Shrine of the Unborn
Pieta
Guided Tours
Spiritual Talks

LANGUAGES

English and Spanish

St. Joseph Proto-Cathedral

ARCHDIOCESE OF LOUISVILLE
310 W. STEPHEN FOSTER AVENUE • BARDSTOWN, KY 40004 • (502) 348-3126

HISTORY OF THE SHRINE

St. Joseph's is the first Proto-Cathedral west of the Allegheny Mountains. The magnificent structure, completed in 1819, rose in the Kentucky wilderness as a monument to the faith, toil, and zeal of a French priest, Benedict Joseph Flaget, who became the first bishop of Bardstown. This historic edifice contains fine paintings, gifts of Francis I, King of the Two Sicilies, and Pope Leo XII. Other gifts came from the nobles of Europe, including King Louis Phillippe of France.

In 1775, Catholic settlers, mostly of English and Irish descent, began emigrating chiefly from Maryland to Kentucky, an outpost of the crown colony of Virginia. The first missionaries came around 1787. In 1808, at the request of Bishop John Carroll of Baltimore, four new Catholic dioceses were created: Bardstown, Boston, New York, and Philadelphia.

In 1811, three years after he was appointed, Bishop Flaget arrived at Bardstown, after traveling down the Ohio River by flatboat and overland from Louisville by wagon, accompanied by a group of seminarians. Bishop Flaget was able to build a small brick church near Bardstown, named St. Thomas. Soon he was consumed with the idea of erecting a cathedral of majestic proportions. Since most of the settlers were very poor, people contributed their materials and their labor as carpenters and masons to build the cathedral. Protestants and Catholics worked together.

After a five-year struggle to get enough money to begin this large undertaking, the cornerstone of the cathedral was laid in 1816. Bricks were baked on the grounds, and solid tree trunks cut from the wilderness were lathed in a circular pattern to form the stately columns supporting the building.

The cathedral was consecrated in 1819, though the interior was not fully completed until 1823. When the Episcopal See was moved forty miles away to the fast-growing city of Louisville in 1841, St. Joseph's became a parish church, hence, the title "proto-cathedral."

SCHEDULE OF MASSES
Sunday Vigil: 5:00 p.m.
Sunday: 7:00 a.m., 9:00 a.m., 11:30 a.m.
Monday–Friday: 6:30 a.m.

Shrine of Mary, Mother of the Church and Model of All Christians

DIOCESE OF OWENSBORO
434 CHURCH STREET • BOWLING GREEN, KY 42101 • (502) 842-2525

HISTORY OF THE SHRINE

The shrine, blessed on May 7, 1989, by Most Rev. John McRaith, is 35′ x 15′ with seating for more than thirty people. Nine stained-glass windows commemorate Cana, Guadalupe, Miraculous Medal, Tri-Millennium 2000, Legion of Mary, La Salette, Lourdes, Fatima, and Tre Fontane. Three large windows in the front commemorate the "Miracle of the Sun" at Fatima. On the other side, three large windows commemorate St. Peter, St. Paul, and the Sacred Heart of Jesus.

The Blessed Sacrament is kept at the shrine, and there is a large statue of Mary.

Catholics and non-Catholics from this community pray daily in the shrine. From time to time there is a pilgrimage from distant parishes.

DEVOTIONS

Rosary: Saturday, 5:00 p.m.
Benediction and Exposition: various times throughout the year

Shrine of Our Lady of Guadalupe

DIOCESE OF LEXINGTON
617 E. MAIN STREET • P.O. BOX 168 • CARLISLE, KY 40311 • (606) 289-5502

HISTORY OF THE SHRINE

The shrine, founded in 1902, was originally known as St. John Church. The church building was constructed in 1906, and a rectory was built next to the church in 1914. The parish struggled to survive during two World Wars and the Great Depression. From 1946 until 1962, it was operated by the Redemptorist Fathers who ran a mission house.

In 1962, Most Rev. Richard H. Ackerman (bishop of Covington), saw the need for a Marian shrine in the diocese. The parish in Carlisle was thus renamed the Shrine of Our Lady of Guadalupe on May 31, 1962. Our Lady of Guadalupe was chosen as patroness because Bishop Ackerman had worked with Hispanic Americans when he was the auxiliary bishop of San Diego in the 1950s. It was hoped that pilgrims would travel to Carlisle to visit their diocesan shrine out of love for Our Lady and, by their generosity, would help the financial plight of the parish through donations.

A new shrine was dedicated on the Feast of the Assumption in 1982, which replaced the original church that had severe structural problems. The shrine has been in the Diocese of Lexington since the new diocese was created in 1988.

The major celebration of the year is a potluck dinner on the Sunday closest to the Feast of Our Lady of Guadalupe.

SCHEDULE OF MASSES
Sunday: 8:30 a.m.

Cathedral Basilica of the Assumption

DIOCESE OF COVINGTON
1140 MADISON AVENUE • COVINGTON, KY 41011 • (606) 431-2060

HISTORY OF THE SHRINE

The Cathedral Basilica of the Assumption, seat of the Catholic Diocese of Covington, is a living monument to the strenuous labors and ardent faith of those who dared to build this edifice of glass. It is an art and architectural monument to be treasured for centuries by people everywhere.

The building of the cathedral was the lifelong dream of Most Rev. Camillus Paul Maes, third bishop of the Diocese of Covington. The dream evolved into a seemingly interminable project, which was begun in 1894.

The basilica, similar to most of the Gothic cathedrals built in the Middle Ages, is dedicated to the Blessed Virgin Mary, or "Our Lady" (Notre Dame), celebrating the human vessel by which Christ became man. The figure of the Madonna and Child strikes the beholder as wonderfully lifelike, and compels one to study and to speculate upon the expressive faces of the Mother and the Infant—the infinite love of Jesus, the cooperation of the Blessed Virgin, and the glory of God.

The majestic north transept window, 64-feet wide, is the largest stained-glass church window in the world. The window presents the early fifth-century Ecumenical Council of Ephesus that proclaimed Mary the Mother of God. The upper tier illustrates the Coronation of the Blessed Virgin Mary as queen of heaven and earth. The massive carved Marian shrine depicts the seven joys and the seven sorrows of the Blessed Mother of Jesus.

Pilgrims and visitors are welcome daily 10:00 a.m.–4:00 p.m. More than ten thousand people come annually on scheduled tours; numerous others come daily to experience the transcendent beauty and presence of God. Parishioners and friends of the cathedral gather on August 15 to celebrate God's goodness and presence among us.

This worthy testimonial of the faith of the people of yesteryear, linked with those who seek a religious awareness of God in today's world, is truly a wonder to behold!

SCHEDULE OF MASSES
Sunday Vigil: 4:30 p.m.
Sunday: 10 a.m., 5:30 p.m.
Daily: 10:00 a.m. (except Thursday and Saturday)
Holy Day of Obligation Vigil: 5:30 p.m.
Holy Day of Obligation: 7:15 a.m., 12:05 p.m.
Reconciliation: Saturday, 3:00 p.m.

DEVOTIONS
Christian Initiation of Adults Program: Weekly
Advent Lessons and Carols: Second Sunday of Advent
Evening Prayer and Speaker: Friday evenings, Lent
Patronal Feastday Celebration: August 15
Concerts of Sacred Music: Monthly on Sundays, 3:00 p.m.

FACILITIES
Gift Shop
Museum
Meditation Gardens
Meeting Room accessible to people with disabilities

LANGUAGES
Some services are signed for the deaf
Brochures in Japanese

The Shrine of St. Ann

DIOCESE OF COVINGTON

ST. ANN'S CHURCH • 1274 PARKWAY • COVINGTON, KY 41011 • (606) 261-9548

HISTORY OF THE SHRINE

Through the efforts of Rev. Louis G. Clermont, relics were secured in 1888 and thus the Shrine of St. Ann was established. On July 18, 1888, a novena was started for nine days ending on July 26—the Feast of Saints Ann and Joachim—with a candlelight procession through the West Covington neighborhood. This tradition continues today.

The shrine draws crowds from all over the Northern Kentucky and Greater Cincinnati, Ohio, area for this novena. Bishop Kendrick Williams (then auxiliary bishop of Covington) celebrated the one hundredth anniversary of the novena on July 26, 1988 with the parishioners of St. Ann and novena participants.

During the nine days of the novena, people can sign up for the St. Ann Pilgrim Society. A donation can be made and a Mass is said every week of the year at the church for all the intentions of the society members.

SCHEDULE OF MASSES
Sunday: 11:00 a.m.
Weekday: 9:30 a.m.

DEVOTIONS
Novena to St. Ann: July 18–26

FACILITIES
Accessible to people with disabilities

The Shrine
of the Little Flower

DIOCESE OF COVINGTON
ST. THERESE CHURCH • 11 TEMPLE PLACE • SOUTHGATE, KY 41071 • (606) 441-1654

HISTORY OF THE SHRINE

In 1927, the Catholic families in the surrounding areas of Southgate, Ky., wanted their own church and school. The bishop of the diocese, aware of the needs of his flock, purchased a piece of property on Alexandria Pike in August 1927. The parish had its beginning.

These Catholic families welcomed the opportunity to work long hours to ready the old building for occupancy. Bishop Francis W. Howard canonically erected the parish on August 15, 1927, the great Feast of the Assumption of Our Lady. He appointed Msgr. Lehr the first pastor. Msgr. Lehr worked side by side with his parishioners to give the new parish a sound foundation to grow and develop.

Enthusiasm intermingled with appreciation became a driving force within the small group to hasten the day of the first Mass in the new church. Using an altar borrowed from the Sisters of the Good Shepherd Convent in Fort Thomas, Ky., the first Mass at the new site was celebrated by Msgr. Lehr on Sunday, August 21, 1927.

On October 2, 1927, Bishop Howard dedicated the new St. Therese Church and School. By the first anniversary of the parish, its growth had exceeded all expectations. The following day, on the Feast of the Little Flower, Bishop Howard declared the new church a diocesan Shrine of the Little Flower. A Perpetual Novena was inaugurated at this shrine in honor of the Little Flower, as were five annual special novena services.

The reliquary includes three first-class relics of St. Therese, one presented to Msgr. Lehr, and two relics from Bishop Howard, as well as a gift from Mother Agnes when the bishop visited Lisieux in the early fall of 1929.

SCHEDULE OF MASSES

Sunday Vigil: 5:00 p.m. (junior choir, first and third Saturdays)
Sunday: 8:00 a.m., 10:15 a.m. (senior choir, first and third Sundays), noon
Daily: 7:00 a.m., 8:15 a.m.
Holy Day of Obligation Vigil: 7:00 p.m.
Holy Day of Obligation: 7:00 a.m., 8:15 a.m., 11:00 a.m., 7:00 p.m.

Shrine of St. John Berchmans

DIOCESE OF LAFAYETTE
1821 ACADEMY ROAD • P.O. BOX 310 • GRAND COTEAU, LA 70541
(318) 662-5494

HISTORY OF THE SHRINE

 In 1866, in the little town of Grand Coteau, La., Blessed John Berchmans appeared to a young novice of the Society of the Sacred Heart. Through the intercession of this Belgian, Mary Wilson was miraculously cured of a disease. The Catholic Church, in accepting this miracle, proclaimed John Berchmans a saint of the Church. He is the patron saint of all altar boys in the Church. The infirmary room where the miracle occurred has been converted into a chapel where hundreds come to pray each year. This shrine is the only place in the United States where the exact spot of a miraculous occurrence has been preserved as a shrine.

The Academy of the Sacred Heart, located on the grounds and founded in 1821, is the oldest continuously operated of the more than two hundred Sacred Heart schools located on five continents around the world.

Tours, lasting about an hour, give the history of the academy, gardens, buildings, shrine, and locations of Civil War battles. The academy and shrine are listed on the National Historical Register.

SCHEDULE OF TOURS
Only upon request

FACILITIES
Museum
Gardens

LANGUAGES
English and French (upon request)

St. Ann National Shrine

ARCHDIOCESE OF NEW ORLEANS
4920 LOVELAND STREET • METAIRIE, LA 70006 • (504) 455-7071 • FAX (504) 455-7076

HISTORY OF THE SHRINE

 The National Shrine of St. Ann was established in the parish of St. Ann, New Orleans, on May 18, 1926. When it became necessary to close the parish of St. Ann, the shrine was transferred to a newly erected parish in Metairie. The church and national shrine were completed in October 1976 and officially dedicated on July 24, 1977.

The stained-glass windows in the church (which are designed in the form of a cross) represent the Joyful, Sorrowful, and Glorious Mysteries of the rosary. The chapels are designated as Our Lady's Chapel, Crucifixion Chapel, and Resurrection Chapel.

The grotto-like structure in the center of the shrine area was designed to approximate the grotto that graced the grounds of the original St. Ann's. It contains the holy stairs, which people may ascend on their knees while meditating on the Stations of the Cross depicted in the beautiful stained-glass window. A large wood-carved crucifix and also the statue of St. Ann are at the top of the stairs. The window facing the north depicts St. Ann, the grandmother of our Savior, and her husband, St. Joachim. These windows are a memorial to the Louisiana Oyster Industry, the fishermen and their families who generously donated to the building and maintenance of these beautiful windows.

SCHEDULE OF MASSES

Sunday Vigil: 4:00 p.m., 5:30 p.m.
Sunday: 8:00 a.m., 9:30 a.m., 11:00 a.m., 12:15 p.m., 5:00 p.m.
Monday–Friday: 6:30 p.m., 8:30 p.m.
Saturday: 7:30 a.m.
Confessions: Saturday, 3:00 p.m.–4:00 p.m., 4:45 p.m.–5:30 p.m.

DEVOTIONS

Novena to St. Ann: Tuesday following 8:30 a.m. Mass and during 7:30 p.m. Mass
Exposition of the Blessed Sacrament: Tuesday, 9:00 a.m.–7:15 p.m.; First Friday, 9:00–11:15 a.m.
Solemn Novenas: Twice each year the shrine conducts a nine-day period of retreat and spiritual renewal: Thursday following Ash Wednesday–Friday of the following week; July 18–Feast of St. Ann, July 26.

FACILITIES

St. Ann Gift Shop

International Shrine of St. Jude

ARCHDIOCESE OF NEW ORLEANS
OUR LADY OF GUADALUPE CHAPEL • 411 N. RAMPART STREET • NEW ORLEANS, LA 70112
(504) 525-1551

HISTORY OF THE SHRINE

 Ecclesiastical permission for the shrine was obtained in 1935, after a group of parishioners had petitions granted through the apostle's intercession. The first solemn novena to St. Jude was inaugurated on January 6, 1935. A small statue and a relic of the apostle Jude were originally placed in a niche in the chapel; as devotions increased, a life-size statue was purchased and was placed in the shrine to the left of the main altar.

The chapel itself is the oldest surviving church in New Orleans and is located on the edge of the historic French Quarter. Built during the yellow-fever epidemic of 1827, the chapel was first used as a mortuary chapel of the cathedral church. In 1865, the chapel provided a gathering place for Confederate veterans. In 1918, care of the chapel was entrusted to the Oblates of Mary Immaculate. The shrine also serves as the memorial chapel for the New Orleans police and fire departments.

Since the first St. Jude devotions in 1935, thousands of people have passed through the doors of the chapel or have attended the solemn novena, seeking the intercession of the apostle known for difficult and apparently impossible cases.

In addition to the Sunday novena to St. Jude, a nine-day solemn novena is held quarterly (during late January, April, July, and October).

SCHEDULE OF MASSES
Sunday Vigil: 4:00 p.m.
Sunday: 7:30 a.m., 9:30 a.m., 11:30 a.m., 6:00 p.m.
Confessions: Saturdays, 3:15–4:00 p.m., during Solemn Novenas, 30 minutes before
each service, and by appointment

DEVOTIONS
Weekly Novena Prayers (after Sunday Masses)
Quarterly Solemn Novenas
Rite of Christian Initiation of Adults
Stations of the Cross (during Lent)
Weekly, Tri-state Radio Broadcasts (daily during Novenas)

FACILITIES
St. Jude Hall
St. Jude Community Center
Gift Shop

LANGUAGES
English and Spanish

National Votive Shrine of Our Lady of Prompt Succor

ARCHDIOCESE OF NEW ORLEANS
2635 STATE STREET • NEW ORLEANS, LA 70118 • (504) 866-1472

HISTORY OF THE SHRINE

 The Ursulines came to New Orleans in 1727, under the auspices of King Louis XV of France, to teach the children of the colonists and to nurse the sick in a military hospital. The statue of Our Lady of Prompt Succor was brought from France by an Ursuline Sister in 1810. In fact, it was this holy nun, Mother St. Michel, who had given Mary this title when she had received a speedy answer to her prayers. Before coming to New Orleans, Mother St. Michel had the special statue made, and she promised Our Lady she would have her honored in New Orleans under the title of Our Lady of Prompt Succor.

History books do not record Mary's role in protecting New Orleans in the battle fought there in 1815. For Catholics of that city, however, it is a well-remembered fact; yearly on January 8, a Mass of Thanksgiving is offered on the anniversary of what is called the Battle of New Orleans.

On the morning of January 8, 1815, the vicar general celebrated Mass on the main altar, above which the statue had been placed. Before the end of Mass, a messenger arrived to announce the end of the battle and the defeat of the British. The battle had lasted less than twenty minutes.

History records that General Jackson went in person to the convent to thank the nuns for their prayers. According to the Ursulines, this was the second time that Our Lady of Prompt Succor had interceded on behalf of New Orleans. In 1812, when a fire was ravaging the city and the wind was driving the flames toward the Ursuline Convent and the nearby buildings, one of the sisters, before fleeing the cloister, placed a small statue of Our Lady of Prompt Succor on a windowsill facing the fire. At the same time, another sister prayed aloud: "Our Lady of Prompt Succor, hasten to our help or we are lost." Scarcely had she uttered the last word when the wind changed direction and the convent was saved. Witnesses attest to the fact.

Pope Pius V authorized the celebration of the Feast of Our Lady of Prompt Succor as well as the signing of the yearly Mass of Thanksgiving on January 8. In 1894, Pope Leo XIII issued a decree granting the "Solemn Coronation of the Miraculous Statue of Our Lady of Prompt Succor, exposed to public veneration in the chapel of the Ursuline Convent, New Orleans."

In June 1928, with the approval of the Holy See, the bishops of the Diocese of Louisiana chose Our Lady of Prompt Succor as Patroness of the City of New Orleans and of the State of Louisiana and designated January 8 as the patronal feast. The statue is venerated in the National Shrine of Our Lady of Prompt Succor, where countless favors have been reported.

SCHEDULE OF MASSES
Masses are scheduled a the beginning of each month.
Masses for special occasions are celebrated with permission.

DEVOTIONS
Peace Mass with Rosary and Confessions: Monthly, 6:00–9:30 p.m.
Passio Domini with Benediction: First Thursday, 9:00 a.m.–noon
Christmas Novena
Feast of Our Lady of Prompt Succor Novena
Solemn Mass of Thanksgiving: January 8, Feast of Our Lady of Prompt Succor

Tours must be made by appointment in advance by letter or telephone.

St. Roch Chapel and the Campo Santo

ARCHDIOCESE OF NEW ORLEANS
1725 ST. ROCH AVENUE • NEW ORLEANS, LA 70117 • (504) 945-5961

HISTORY OF THE SHRINE

 St. Roch was born in 1295 in Montpellier, France. Deeply religious, he went to Rome and devoted himself to caring for those stricken by the Black Plague. It is said that through his prayers, Rome was spared from the plague. He returned to Montpellier after seven years but was accused of being a spy and was sent to prison for five years. He died there, and it is said a bright light shone around him at the time of his death. Many miracles have occurred attesting to his sanctity; he is known as the saint to invoke in cases of affliction, disease, and deformities.

In 1867, in New Orleans, Fr. Thevis of Holy Trinity Church appealed to St. Roch that his parishioners be spared during an outbreak of yellow fever. Supposedly, none of them died, so Fr. Thevis fulfilled his promise of erecting a chapel and cemetery in honor of the saint. On September 6, 1875, the cemetery (Campo Santo) was dedicated, and the cornerstone of the chapel was laid. The chapel and shrine were dedicated on August 16, 1876, feast of the saint. People began to flock to the site, especially on his feast day, All Saints Day, All Souls Day, and Good Friday.

Many have attested to being cured through the intercession of St. Roch. In a little room to the side of the chapel sanctuary lies a collection of crutches and braces—objects that graphically express the thanks of clients of St. Roch for favors obtained.

SCHEDULE OF MASSES
Every Monday morning

DEVOTIONS
Feast of St. Roch: August 16 (Services are held for nine days before his feast)
Good Friday: Way of the Cross, 3:00 p.m.
All Saints Day: Pilgrimage to Campo Santo, Way of the Cross

National Shrine of the Infant Jesus of Prague

ARCHDIOCESE OF OKLAHOMA CITY
P.O. BOX 488 • PRAGUE, OK 74864 • (405) 567-3080

HISTORY OF THE SHRINE

The Catholic people of Prague, Okla., first worshiped in a small wooden church under the patronage of St. Wenceslaus. As the Catholic population grew, there was need for a larger church; new churches were built in 1909 and 1919. From 1947 to 1949, a church was built under the guidance of the pastor, Fr. George V. Johnson, who credited the accomplishment of the construction of the church to the Infant Jesus of Prague. Planning for the new church had begun in 1945, and although aspirations were high, it seemed as if a new church was many years in the future because of lack of finances. Fr. Johnson promised that he would make the church a shrine to the Infant Jesus of Prague if the Infant Jesus would help him get the new church built. Donations of money and supplies soon started arriving from parishioners and businesses in Prague and even from other individuals throughout the United States. As a result, the new church was dedicated under the patronage of St. Wenceslaus on February 22, 1949. Keeping his promise, Fr. Johnson set a statue of the Infant Jesus of Prague "on a throne of gold" behind the main altar.

Permission was given from Rome by the Carmelite General on August 16, 1949, to establish the Association of the Infant Jesus of Prague in St. Wenceslaus Catholic Church, Prague, Okla.

Since this time, people from around the world have been accepted into the Association of the Infant Jesus of Prague at Prague, Okla. Public devotions to the Infant Jesus of Prague have been offered at this U.S. shrine, which has been a national shrine since its establishment in 1949.

SCHEDULE OF MASSES

Sunday Vigil: 6:00 p.m.
Sunday: 7:30 a.m., 11:00 a.m.
Holy Day of Obligation: 7:00 a.m., 7:30 p.m.

DEVOTIONS

Novena to the Infant Jesus of Prague: The 17th–25th of each month

FACILITIES

Gift Shop: Weekdays, 9:00 a.m.–4:00 p.m.

Shrine of Our Lady Virgin of the Poor

DIOCESE OF KNOXVILLE

P.O. BOX 288 • SOUTH PITTSBURG, TN 37380 • LOCATED IN NEW HOPE, TENN.

(423) 837-7068

HISTORY OF THE SHRINE

The Shrine of Our Lady Virgin of the Poor is a replica of the original shrine in Banneaux, Belgium, which marks the site of a 1933 apparition of Mary. This shrine is the creation of Fr. Basil Mattingly, a Benedictine monk.

Mary appeared eight times in Banneaux, between January and March, to Marietta Beco, an 11-year old peasant girl. Mary asked that a little chapel be built in her honor and that people would come and pray in procession, especially the rosary. She called herself the Virgin of the Poor. A small chapel was built beside a spring that appeared during one of the apparitions, and it was blessed August 15, 1933. Bishop Louis J. Kerkofs of Liege gave his approval to devotion to Our Lady of Banneaux in 1949.

While more than one hundred sanctuaries throughout the world are dedicated to Our Lady of Banneaux, Our Lady Virgin of the Poor is the only one in the United States. The shrine itself is small and simple, as Mary requested. It is almost identical to its Belgian model, but the materials are distinctly from the Tennessee area. The stone for the walls and massive altar came from a nearby quarry, and the iron gates were designed and built by a local ironworker.

People from all over the Chattanooga area visit this shrine, with some traveling from Nashville, Alabama, and Georgia, to be renewed and spiritually refreshed.

DEVOTIONS

Sundays in May and October, 2:00 p.m. (Central Time)

La Promesa—Shrine to Our Lady of Guadalupe, Empress of the Americas

DIOCESE OF SAN ANGELO
1401 E. GARDEN LANE • P.O. BOX 7 • MIDLAND, TX 79701
(915) 682-2581 • FAX (915) 682-9364

HISTORY OF THE SHRINE

The vision to build a shrine to Our Lady of Guadalupe came as a result of the parish community being called to prayer. It all came about from the faith of the people. In January 1986, Fr. Jimmy Norman, OMI (d. 1986) and Fr. Domingo Estrada, OMI, were assigned to Our Lady of Guadalupe Parish in Midland, Texas. The people were deeply concerned over the frightening situations that beset them. Many youth had openly abandoned their faith, in search of easy money, quick success, and endless pleasure. Abortion, disregard for life, suicide among the youth, and a clear disdain for God were all part of the dark picture. The drug culture fueled this poisoned atmosphere, leaving untold victims in its path. Great numbers of people were left unemployed by the drastic collapse of the oil business, backbone of the West Texas economy. The only hope was to seek divine intervention.

Out of the sacrificial prayer came the "vision": To raise a banner to Our Lady of Guadalupe and answer her desire to come to her in our trouble, she who brought millions into the living stream of Catholicism, out of pagan darkness. Great devotion and frequent pilgrimages made to Our Lady of Guadalupe resulted in a promise made by the people to develop the sacred site, to accommodate many pilgrims who spontaneously seek the protection of Our Lady of Guadalupe.

With 3,000 pilgrims attending, the first phase of this beautiful outdoor parish shrine was dedicated by Most Rev. Michael D. Pfeifer, OMI, bishop of San Angelo, on June 8, 1993. Now that the second phase of construction has been completed, it has a seating capacity of 2,642 plus ample space for standing. The majestic statue of Our Lady of Guadalupe is made of bronze and stands nine feet tall and captivates the minds and hearts of people who seek conversion and the grace of God to continue life's journey.

SCHEDULE OF MASSES

Sunday Vigil: 5:00 p.m. (Spanish)

Sunday: 8:00 a.m. (Spanish), 10:00 a.m., noon (English)

Daily: Monday–Friday, 6:30 a.m. (Bilingual); Lunes, Miercoles, Jueves, 7:00 p.m. (Spanish); Tuesday and Friday, 7:00 p.m. (English); Saturday, 8:00 a.m. (Bilingual)

Confessions: Weekday, 6:30 p.m.; Saturday, 3:00–5:00 p.m.

DEVOTIONS

Perpetual Adoration

First Fridays

First Saturdays

Youth Prayer Meeting, Sundays, 6:00 p.m.

Adult Spanish Prayer Meeting, Mondays following 7:00 p.m. Mass

FACILITIES

Gift Shop

LANGUAGES

English and Spanish

National Shrine of the Little Flower

ARCHDIOCESE OF SAN ANTONIO
906 KENTUCKY AVENUE • P.O. BOX 5280 • SAN ANTONIO, TX 78201 • (210) 735-9126

HISTORY OF THE SHRINE

The National Shrine of the Little Flower serves as a parish church for two thousand Roman Catholics. It was built and is directed by the Discalced Carmelite Fathers. The shrine's massive exterior is made from Indiana limestone; the front is flanked by two massive towers, one of which contains six bells that weigh a total of eight thousand pounds. Centered above the middle of the shrine is a dome 32 feet in diameter and rising to a height of 70 feet.

The Carmelites arrived in this country early this century after being exiled following the bloody battle for Torreon during the revolution. They first became established in Oklahoma and, in 1923, were asked by the archbishop of San Antonio to establish a parish there and to give his people spiritual help. With some difficulties, the Carmelites finally dedicated a church there on August 29, 1926. This building was used to celebrate Mass for the next two years.

In 1927, a plan for the Shrine of St. Therese was conceived. Archbishop Arthur J. Drossaerts gave the Carmelite Fathers his blessing, and the order began its campaign for funds for the new church. People around the world responded to their appeal and, in the fall of 1931, the present building was dedicated to St. Therese by the Most Rev. José Jesus Manriquez, bishop of Huejtla, Mexico.

The shrine celebrated its fiftieth anniversary in 1981. Since its beginning, the shrine has been a site of devotion to the Little Flower and of pilgrimage from throughout the nation and beyond. Those who visit the shrine marvel at the beauty of the architecture, the artistry of the mosaic covered marble altars, and the vivid color of the stained-glass windows. Shrine visitors are spiritually elevated by the devotional treasures the shrine safeguards, such as a 10' x 7' painting of St. Therese worked on by Sr. Celine, St. Therese's blood sister. This painting was used for the canonization ceremonies of St. Therese in 1925.

From October 1, 1996 through October 1, 1997, the shrine celebrated the Centenary (100th anniversary) of the death of St. Therese. During that year, the Carmelites began a second national campaign and a restoration project to bring the shrine back to its original glory.

SCHEDULE OF MASSES
Sunday: 8:00 a.m., 9:30 a.m., 11:00 a.m., 12:30 p.m.
Weekday: 8:15 a.m. (8:00 a.m. during summer), 5:30 p.m.
Saturday: 8:00 a.m., 5:30 p.m.

DEVOTIONS
Perpetual Mass Association: Daily Mass celebrated for all enrolled
Perpetual Novena to St. Therese: Tuesdays after 5:30 p.m. Mass
Yearly Novena anticipating the Feast of St. Therese: September 23–28
Solemn Triduum: September 29, 30, and October 1
Solemnity of St. Teresa of Avila: October 15 (Special Sung Mass)
Solemnity of St. John of the Cross: December 14 (Special Sung Mass)

LANGUAGES
English and Spanish

Our Lady of San Juan del Valle Shrine

DIOCESE OF BROWNSVILLE
400 N. NEBRASKA • P.O. BOX 747 • SAN JUAN, TX 78589
(210) 787-0033 • FAX (210) 787-2908

HISTORY OF THE SHRINE

The history of the Virgen de San Juan Shrine has its roots in the religious experience of a people who have felt the very close presence of Mary, the Mother of God. In 1623, through Mary's intercession, a young girl was brought back to life. Mary then became known as *La Virgen de San Juan de los Lagos*. This story filled the Mexican town with deep feelings of thanksgiving and confidence to *La Virgen* who took such great care of them.

In 1949, Fr. José Maria Azpiazu, OMI, aware of the devotion of Mexican Americans to Mary, placed a replica of the statue of *La Virgen de San Juan de los Lagos* in his parish church of St. John the Baptist, San Juan, Texas. As the number of pilgrims grew, Fr. José decided to build a shrine, which was officially dedicated on May 2, 1954.

The original shrine was destroyed in 1970 as a result of a plane crash. On April 19, 1980, a new, spacious, and modern shrine, able to seat three thousand visitors, was dedicated. It features a 40' x 30' Italian mosaic. Life-size bronze Stations of the Cross are placed on an outside walk.

SCHEDULE OF MASSES

(All Masses are in Spanish unless otherwise noted.)
Saturday: 6:30 a.m., 9:30 a.m., 11:30 a.m.; Vigil: 5:30 p.m. (English)
Sunday: 6:30 a.m., 8:30 a.m., 10:30 a.m. (Bilingual), 12:30 p.m., 5:30 p.m.
Daily: 6:30 a.m., 11:30 a.m., 5:30 p.m.
Holy Day of Obligation: 6:30 a.m., 9:30 a.m., 11:30 a.m., 5:30 p.m.
Confessions: Available throughout the day

DEVOTIONS
Rosary: Daily
Stations of the Cross

NOVENAS
Feast of Our Lady of San Juan: January 25–February 2
Easter Novena
Mother's Day Novena
Father's Day Novena
Assumption of Our Lady: August 7–15
All Souls Novena
Christmas Novena

FACILITIES
Religious Gift and Bookstore
Pilgrim House (overnight accommodations)
Cafeteria
Retreat House
Nursing Home

LANGUAGES
English and Spanish

Southeast

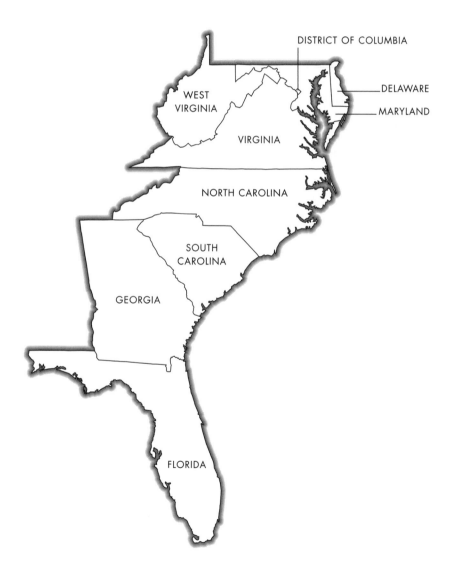

DISTRICT OF COLUMBIA

DELAWARE

MARYLAND

WEST
VIRGINIA

VIRGINIA

NORTH CAROLINA

SOUTH
CAROLINA

GEORGIA

FLORIDA

St. Francis Xavier Shrine

DIOCESE OF WILMINGTON
(OLD BOHEMIA) WARWICK, MD
C/O ST. JOSEPH'S CHURCH • 15 W. COCHRAN STREET • P.O. BOX 196
MIDDLETOWN, DE 19709 • (302) 378-1939

HISTORY OF THE SHRINE

In 1704, the Jesuits founded St. Francis Xavier as the center for new mission activity east of the Chesapeake Bay. The original boundaries of its mission activity included the present Diocese of Wilmington and the Archdiocese of Philadelphia.

After the parish seat was moved to Middletown, Del., in 1908, St. Francis Xavier was continued as a mission, but after 1929 only annual field Masses were celebrated at Old Bohemia.

Following World War II, an upsurge of interest in the pioneer parish of the Wilmington diocese led to the formation of the Old Bohemia Historical Society, which restored and now maintains the old church as a historic shrine for the diocese. It commemorates the missionary spirit of St. Francis Xavier and his Jesuit successors, who first planted the seeds of faith within the bounds of the present Diocese of Wilmington.

SCHEDULE OF MASSES

Fourth Sunday of April, May, September, and October: 4:00 p.m.
(When Easter falls on the fourth Sunday, the April pilgrimage is held on the third Sunday.)

Basilica of the National Shrine of the Immaculate Conception

ARCHDIOCESE OF WASHINGTON
FOURTH STREET AND MICHIGAN AVENUE NE • WASHINGTON DC 20017-1566
(202) 526-8300 • INTERNET: WWW.NATIONALSHRINE.COM

HISTORY OF THE SHRINE

 The Basilica of the National Shrine is the largest Roman Catholic church in the Western Hemisphere and the eighth largest church in the world. The idea of a national shrine was conceived in the early 1900s by Bishop Thomas J. Shahan, the fourth rector of The Catholic University of America. Under his direction, the Crypt Church was completed and the foundation begun; however, because of the Great Depression, financial contributions and all construction ceased. Thus, the project of building the shrine would lay dormant for almost twenty-five years.

After World War II, Archbishop John Noll of Fort Wayne, Ind., Archbishop Patrick O'Boyle of Washington, D.C., and Mr. James J. Norris of New York, rekindled the dream of the shrine. In 1953, they gained the support of the U.S. Catholic bishops, who then elicited and received funds from every parish in the country as well as from the Knights of Columbus. Construction resumed in 1954; by 1959, the Great Upper Church was completed and dedicated.

The Basilica of the National Shrine, designed in the Byzantine-Romanesque style, contains sixty chapels displaying a wide variety of stained glass, mosaics, and sculpture. Each chapel and piece of artwork in the shrine encompasses the history of Catholic devotion to Mary. This shrine is unique among all others in the country because it is the national church for all Catholics who come each year to honor Mary and to renew their faith through worship to God.

The shrine is open November 1–March 31, 7:00 a.m.–6:00 p.m.; and
April 1–October 31, 7:00 a.m.–7:00 p.m.

SCHEDULE OF MASSES

Sunday Vigil: 5:15 p.m.

Sunday: 9:00 a.m., 10:30 a.m., noon, 4:30 p.m. (Great Upper Church); 7:30 a.m.,
1:30 p.m. (Crypt Church)

Weekday: 7:00 a.m., 7:30 a.m., 8:00 a.m., 8:30 a.m.; 12:10 p.m., 5:15 p.m.
(Crypt Church)

Holy Day of Obligation Vigil: 5:30 p.m.

Holy Day of Obligation: 7:00 a.m., 7:30 a.m., 8:00 a.m., 8:30 a.m., 10:00 a.m.,
noon, 5:30 p.m.

Confessions: Monday–Saturday, 7:45–8:15 a.m., 10:00 a.m.–noon, 3:30–6:00 p.m.;
Sunday, 10:00 a.m.–noon; 2:00–4:00 p.m.

DEVOTIONS

Rosary: Weekday, 11:50 a.m., 4:50 p.m.; Sunday, 1:10 p.m.

FACILITIES

Gift Shop
Bookstore
Cafeteria
Guided Tours

Franciscan Monastery (Holy Land of America)

ARCHDIOCESE OF WASHINGTON
1400 QUINCY STREET NE • WASHINGTON DC 20017 • (202) 526-6800

HISTORY OF THE SHRINE

The Franciscans have a long history in the Holy Land as guardians of the Holy Sepulchre. They witnessed firsthand the importance of pilgrimages to the Holy Land in keeping the faith alive. The order was then given the privilege of establishing a shrine in Washington, D.C. to Our Lord, reproducing many of the sites associated with his life.

Fr. Godfrey Schilling, OFM, founded the monastery/shrine in the late 1800s and opened it to pilgrims in 1898. He named the shrine the Holy Land of America. The shrine is for people who are unable to visit the sacred shrines in the Holy Land. Many shrines and grottoes in the church have been faithfully reproduced according to the originals. These include the Holy Sepulchre, the Sanctuary of Calvary, the Grottoes of Nazareth and Bethlehem, and the Martyrs' Crypt. Outdoor shrines include the Valley and Grotto of Gethsemane, the Tomb of the Blessed Virgin, and the Lourdes Grotto.

The church was constructed in the Byzantine style. The main structure of the church contains a large cross, fifteen chapels, and many smaller crosses. The emblem of the fivefold cross, representing the five wounds of Christ, is found throughout the church, establishing its connection to the Holy Land.

The main religious celebrations are Christmas, Holy Week, Easter, and the Feasts of St. Francis and St. Anthony of Padua. About 60,000 pilgrims visit the shrine annually.

SCHEDULE OF MASSES

Sunday Vigil: 5:00 p.m.
Sunday: 7:00 a.m., 8:30 a.m., 10:30 a.m., noon
Holy Day of Obligation Vigil: 5:00 p.m.
Holy Day of Obligation: 6:00 a.m., 7:00 a.m., 8:00 a.m., 9:00 a.m.
Confessions: Daily, 9:00 a.m., 10:00 a.m., 11:00 a.m., 1:00–4:00 p.m.;
　　　Sunday, 1:00–4:00 p.m.

DEVOTIONS
Novenas: Weekly (St. Anthony)

FACILITIES
Gift Shop

Ukrainian National Shrine of the Holy Family

METROPOLITAN ARCHDIOCESE OF PHILADELPHIA, UKRAINIAN
4250 HAREWOOD ROAD NE • WASHINGTON DC 20017 • (202) 526-3737

HISTORY OF THE SHRINE

Our Holy Family Ukrainian Catholic Church, with the help of 210 Catholic parishes in the United States, built this shrine to commemorate the millennium of Christianity among the Ukrainian people. The icons of the Blessed Virgin Mary of Pochayiv are revered in the shrine and grotto. The grotto also contains a 70-foot cross.

Devotion has been paid to the traveling icon of Pochayiv in the parish since 1977, and pilgrimages began in 1980. The shrine caters to special groups—schoolchildren, youth groups, senior citizens—as well as to individuals, of any denomination.

SCHEDULE OF MASSES
Sunday: 9:30 a.m. (English), 11:15 a.m. (Ukrainian)
Saturday: 9:00 a.m. (English)
Weekdays: 8:00 a.m. (English)
Confessions: Upon request

DEVOTIONS
Prayer Services: Devotion to the Blessed Virgin Mary of Pochayiv
Missions
Retreats

LANGUAGES
English and Ukrainian

Shrine of
Our Lady of Charity

ARCHDIOCESE OF MIAMI
3609 S. MIAMI AVENUE • MIAMI, FL 33133
(305) 854-2404 • (305) 854-2405 • FAX (305) 854-8022

HISTORY OF THE SHRINE

The shrine was commissioned by Archbishop Coleman F. Carroll of Miami, who asked the Cuban people to build a shrine to honor their patroness. A statue of the Virgin, found in the Bay of Nipe in Cuba at the beginning of the seventeenth century, was to be placed in the shrine. In 1967, a small chapel was erected which was to serve as a convent for the Sisters of Charity who work at the shrine.

The present building stands 90 feet high with a width of 80 feet. Built in the shape of a mantle, the temple invites people to enter within the heart of the Virgin so that they may find the Word of God that lives there.

The statue of Our Lady holding out Jesus in her hands is an invitation for the faithful to enter into communion with him through the sacraments of penance and the eucharist.

The Marian shrine was designed and built by Cuban refugees. John Cardinal Krol of Philadelphia dedicated it on December 2, 1973. The shrine stands as a monument to the religious faith of the Cuban people and their commitment to freedom.

Pilgrimages of members of the 126 Cuban municipalities are scheduled throughout the year as well as six picnics for the six Cuban provinces. The month of October is dedicated to the different advocations of the Blessed Mother and to the people of South and Central American nations who live in the area. Mass each evening is dedicated to one nation. September 8 is the main feast celebrated at the shrine.

SCHEDULE OF MASSES

Sunday Vigil: 8:00 p.m.
Holy Day of Obligation Vigil: 8:00 p.m.
Holy Day of Obligation: 8:00 p.m.
Confessions: At anytime

DEVOTIONS

Rosary: Daily
Bible Class: For adults by correspondence
Christian Initiation Program for Adults: Weekly
Feast of Our Lady of Charity: September 8

FACILITIES

Counseling Center

LANGUAGES

Spanish, English, and French

Mary, Queen of the Universe Shrine

DIOCESE OF ORLANDO
8300 VINELAND AVENUE • ORLANDO, FL 32821 • (407) 239-6600

HISTORY OF THE SHRINE

 The shrine is located in the vicinity of Lake Buena Vista, close to Walt Disney World in the Diocese of Orlando.

Commissioned by Bishop Thomas J. Grady in 1984, the preliminary structure opened to the public on April 2, 1986. In late November of that year, papal Pro-Nuncio Pio Laghi, together with the bishops of Florida, officially blessed the new shrine project.

The successor bishop, Most Rev. Norbert Dorsey, CP, enthusiastically promoted the development of the main shrine church, which was begun August 22, 1990. On August 22, 1993, Bishop Dorsey presided at the dedication of the completed edifice with dignitaries from the United States and abroad.

The church features outstanding artwork and a variety of magnificent artistic glass, stained and otherwise. A mosaic of Our Lady of Guadalupe, Queen of the Americas graces the day chapel, already known for its celebrated stained-glass windows. The paintings of the Stations of the Cross, works of art by Franz Ansele, Ghent, 1821, are also noteworthy.

Standing within the shrine grounds is the magnificent Mother and Child Outdoor Chapel. The statuary sculpted by renowned artist Jerzy Kenar stands in tribute to the Incarnation and as a beautiful reminder of the gift of life. Tranquil grounds, flowing fountains, and the Rosary Gardens centered by a historic statue of Mary holding the Divine Infant, complete the prayerful atmosphere.

In 1997, a statue of Mary, Queen of the Universe, by sculptor Jill Burkee, took its place to the right of the sanctuary area of the shrine church. The statue is sculpted in Carrara marble.

The shrine's main emphasis is on evangelization. A museum of religious art and a computerized audiovisual theater will join the religious gift shop and bookstore, completing the evangelization center.

The shrine celebrates its name day on August 22, Feast of the Queenship of Mary.

SCHEDULE OF MASSES

Sunday Vigil: 6:00 p.m.
Sunday: 7:30 a.m., 9:30 a.m., 11:30 a.m., 6:00 p.m.
Daily: 8:00 a.m.
Confessions: Daily, 10:00 a.m.–5:00 p.m.

Shrine of Our Lady of La Leche

DIOCESE OF ST. AUGUSTINE
30 OCEAN AVENUE • ST. AUGUSTINE, FL 32084 • (904) 824-3045

HISTORY OF THE SHRINE

 In 1565, Pedro Menendez founded the Mission of Nombre de Dios and the city of St. Augustine. In 1615, the early Spanish settlers established the first shrine in the United States to be dedicated to the Blessed Virgin Mary as a sign of their love for the Nursing Mother of Christ. They did so on the spot where the first parish Mass had been offered by Fr. Francisco Lopez de Mendoza Grajales, fifty-five years before at the Mission of Nombre de Dios in St. Augustine. The present chapel is the result of restoration begun in 1915. It enshrines a replica of the original statue.

Thousands of mothers visit the shrine every year to ask for the blessings of motherhood, beseeching the intercession of Our Lady of La Leche that God will grant them a safe, happy delivery and healthy, holy children.

The principal memorials are the Chapel of Our Lady of La Leche, the Prince of Peace Church, an 11-foot bronze statue of Fr. Lopez, a 208-foot stainless steel cross, a rustic altar, and a bronze plaque memorializing 45 of the major missions of the First Spanish Period (1565–1763). These missions extended from what is now Miami to the Chesapeake Bay and from the Atlantic Ocean westward to Pensacola.

The annual pilgrimage Mass is celebrated outdoors at the rustic altar on the Saturday closest to September 8, the Feast of Our Lady's Birthday.

SCHEDULE OF MASSES

Sunday Vigil: 6:00 p.m.
Sunday: 8:00 a.m.
Monday–Friday: 8:30 a.m.
Holy Day of Obligation: 8:30 a.m.

DEVOTIONS
Novenas: Tuesday after Mass
Rosary: Before the daily Mass

FACILITIES
Religious Bookstore
Gift Shop
Church Supplies

Basilica of the National Shrine of the Assumption of the Blessed Virgin Mary

ARCHDIOCESE OF BALTIMORE
CATHEDRAL AND MULBERRY STREETS • BALTIMORE, MD 21201 • (410) 727-3564

HISTORY OF THE SHRINE

The history of the Basilica of the Assumption of the Blessed Virgin Mary is intimately tied to that of the Archdiocese of Baltimore; it is indeed integral to the history of the Church in America. The Basilica is the first cathedral in the United States and the mother church of Catholicism in the nation. The decree establishing Baltimore as our first diocese by Pope Pius VI on November 7, 1789, commissioned the first bishop, John Carroll, "to erect a church in the vicinity of the said city of Baltimore in the form of a cathedral church, in as much as the times and circumstances allow."

Even though the status of the diocese demanded a cathedral, Carroll was unable to start the project until 1806. He chose Benjamin H. Latrobe, who was also responsible for the design of the U.S. Treasury Building and the U.S. Capitol. Evoking the style of the ancient roman basilica, Carroll and Latrobe designed and built a truly magnificent cathedral for the first diocese in the United States.

This great cathedral was the site of the first seven provincial councils and three plenary councils in our country. It has witnessed the consecration of many of the first bishops of the Church in the United States. Here, Cardinal James Gibbons (1877–1921) ordained more than 2,400 to the priesthood.

Throughout these events, the protecting mantle of the Blessed Virgin Mary has been ever present in the spirit and devotion of the mother diocese: John Carroll was consecrated first bishop of Baltimore on August 15, 1790. During the Synod of Baltimore (1791), among the twenty-four promulgated statutes was the declaration of the Blessed Virgin Mary as patroness of the diocese and the fixing of August 15, the Feast of the Assumption, as the principal feast day of the diocese.

In 1846, at the Sixth Provincial Council, the bishops petitioned the Holy See to have the Blessed Virgin Mary designated as patroness of the United States under the title of the Immaculate Conception. At the Seventh Provincial Council (1849), the bishops petitioned Pius IX to define the Immaculate Conception of the Virgin Mary, helping pave the way for its declaration as a dogma of the Church.

More recently, the basilica was honored by a visit of His Holiness, Pope John Paul II in October 1995. This special pilgrimage was made in acknowledgment of the great historic significance held by the first cathedral of our nation.

The Archdiocese of Baltimore considers itself fortunate, indeed, for the role played by the basilica in the history of Baltimore, Maryland, the United States, and the Catholic faith.

SCHEDULE OF MASSES
Sunday Vigil: 5:30 p.m. (with music)
Sunday: 7:30 a.m., 9:00 a.m. (Latin), 10:45 a.m. (Choir), 4:00 p.m., 5:30 p.m.
    (with music)
Monday–Friday: 7:30 a.m., 12:10 p.m.
Saturday: 7:30 a.m.
Holy Day of Obligation Vigil: 5:30 p.m.
Holy Day of Obligation: 7:30 a.m., 12:10 p.m.
Confessions: Daily

DEVOTIONS
Exposition of the Blessed Sacrament: Friday, 12:30–3:45 p.m.
Public Recitation of the Rosary: Saturday, 5:00 p.m.
Stations of the Cross: Fridays of Lent, 3:00 p.m.
Holy Week Services
Feast of the Assumption, August 15

FACILITIES
Crypt
Religious Articles and Gift Shop: Monday–Friday, 10:00 a.m.–4:00 p.m.;
    Saturday, 10:00 a.m.–5:30 p.m.; Sunday, 8:00 a.m.–5:30 p.m.
Guided Tours: Each Sunday following the 10:45 a.m. Mass (around noon) and
    by appointment

St. Jude Shrine

ARCHDIOCESE OF BALTIMORE
309 N. PACA STREET • BALTIMORE, MD 21201 • (410) 685-3063

HISTORY OF THE SHRINE

St. Jude Parish was entrusted to the Pallottines by the archbishop of Baltimore in 1917. Around the outset of World War II, devotion to St. Jude was reaching meaningful proportions in the parish, and so it was decided that a shrine should be established in his honor and that novena services should be scheduled on a regular basis.

Interest in the shrine and the services grew so rapidly that it became necessary to initiate mailings in order to answer inquiries and to respond to requests regarding the offering of Masses of petitions and/or thanksgiving to St. Jude. Mailings extended beyond the boundaries of the State of Maryland in 1953. To keep pace with the growing demand of the devotees of St. Jude, three solemn novenas throughout the year were instituted, as were regular weekly services.

Pallottine priests and brothers offer daily prayers in response to the many requests and petitions. It is always of great interest to the Pallottines, in line with the furtherance of the devotion to St. Jude, to know of the many favors that have been received through his intercession. The Pallottine priests and brothers who labor at the shrine respond to the many letters and calls from devotees of St. Jude and conduct the various novenas and other religious services at the shrine.

Today St. Jude's body rests in a tomb in the Vatican Basilica of St. Peter's. This Baltimore shrine has arranged to have a daily Mass celebrated on the altar above the tomb for the intentions of those whose names are registered at the shrine.

SCHEDULE OF MASSES

Sunday: 8:00 a.m., 9:00 a.m., 11:30 a.m.
Wednesday: 7:00 a.m., 12:05 p.m.
Daily: 12:05 p.m.
Saturday: 7:45 a.m.
Confessions: Fifteen minutes before all services

NOVENAS TO ST. JUDE

Sunday: Following the 9:00 a.m. and 11:30 a.m. Masses
Wednesday: 7:45 a.m. (Novena and Mass), noon (Novena and Mass),
    5:45 p.m. (Novena and Benediction), 7:45 p.m. (Novena and Benediction)

Basilica of the National Shrine of St. Elizabeth Ann Seton

ARCHDIOCESE OF BALTIMORE
333 S. SETON AVENUE • EMMITSBURG, MD 21727-9298 • (301) 447-6606

HISTORY OF THE SHRINE

The National Shrine of St. Elizabeth Ann Seton is a beautiful, peaceful shrine built in honor of America's first native-born saint, Elizabeth Ann Bayley Seton (1774–1821). Her shrine is located in Emmitsburg, a small historic town in the foothills of the Catoctin Mountains, 25 miles north of Frederick on U.S. 15 North, left on S. Seton Avenue, or 10 miles south of Gettysburg on U.S. 15 South, right on S. Seton Avenue.

"Mother Seton," as the widow of William Magee Seton and the mother of five children, came to Emmitsburg, Md. in the summer of 1809 with sixteen companions where she established the Sisters of Charity, the first community of women religious founded in this country. On January 4, 1821, Mother Seton died in the white house in the valley she loved. On September 14, 1975, Pope Paul VI proclaimed Elizabeth Ann Seton a saint—the first American-born citizen to be given this honor by the Catholic Church.

Shrine sites include the splendid basilica, which contains the altar of the relics of St. Elizabeth Ann Seton; the original stone house (c. 1750), where she established her religious community in 1809; and the white house (1810), where she began the Catholic Parochial School System in 1810. A visit here includes a 15-minute slide presentation of historical background; a self-guided tour of the other sites includes the mortuary chapel (1846) and cemetery, visitor center, museum, and the religious gift shop. Docent guides are on duty at each site to offer information and answer questions concerning that particular site.

A visit to the Shrine of St. Elizabeth Ann Seton calls attention not only to her heroic life of charity but also to the deeper reality that God was with her, that her daily spiritual life brought her into loving touch with her God. Shrine sites are open seven days a week, 10:00 a.m.–4:30 p.m. Closed Mondays, November 1–March 31, last two weeks in January, Christmas, New Year's, Easter, and Thanksgiving.

Group tours welcome; call (301) 447-6606.

SCHEDULE OF MASSES
Saturday and Sunday: 9:00 a.m.

DEVOTIONS
Daily: Novena prayers to St. Elizabeth Ann Seton

FACILITIES
Visitor Center
Museum
Religious Gift Shop: Accessible to people with disabilities

YEAR 2000
Various celebrations will be held throughout the year in honor of the
25th anniversary of St. Elizabeth Ann Seton's canonization. The anniversary Mass
will be held in September 2000.

National Shrine Grotto of Lourdes

ARCHDIOCESE OF BALTIMORE
MOUNT ST. MARY'S COLLEGE • EMMITSBURG, MD 21727 • (301) 447-5318

HISTORY OF THE SHRINE

Above the lovely valley of Emmitsburg, Md., situated high on a mountainside overlooking Mount St. Mary's campus and the Shrine of St. Elizabeth Ann Seton, a statue of Our Lady rises atop the Pangborn Memorial Campanile.

Fr. John DuBois, a refugee priest from France, came to the Emmitsburg area. The priest, who later became the third bishop of New York, was appointed pastor of Frederick by Bishop John Carroll. Fr. DuBois found the grotto site, in a small wooded valley, of breathtaking beauty. He also found a natural amphitheater where nature "displayed itself in all its wild and picturesque beauty."

A great statue of the Blessed Mother presides over the Valley of St. Mary from her mountain. The melody of the bells, ringing out the Angelus and sacred hymns, call all minds and hearts to Jesus through Mary. Fr. DuBois built his church on this lofty site in order that the people in the valley, during their daily tasks, would look up, would see the cross and their Blessed Mother, and would "keep the faith." This campanile perpetuates the holy purpose of the founder.

In addition to the campanile and grotto lie an exquisite rosary walk and the Stations of the Cross. More than one million pilgrims journey to the grotto each year to refresh their souls and to enliven their faith in God.

It has been said of the National Shrine Grotto of Lourdes that, even though Our Lady never appeared in Emmitsburg, it would be worth a trip from the other side of the world just to see the natural beauty of the spot. The same is true of the mountain grotto.

SCHEDULE OF MASSES
Sunday: noon, 5:00 p.m.

DEVOTIONS

Novena to Our Lady of Lourdes: Sunday, 3:00 p.m., with a homily and benediction.

Anointing of the Sick: After all services at the grotto.

Ecumenical Easter Sunday Sunrise Service: 6:30 a.m., followed by Mass at 7:30 a.m. (This event attracts people of all faiths.)

Medjugorje Day: June 25

Anniversary of Our Lady of Fatima: July 20–21

Annual Novena to Our Lady of the Assumption: August 7–15

Feast of Our Lady of the Assumption: August 15, Solemn Mass with a special speaker each year

Feast of the Holy Angels: October 2

Basilica of St. Mary of the Immaculate Conception

DIOCESE OF RICHMOND
232 CHAPEL STREET • NORFOLK, VA 23504 • (804) 622-4487

HISTORY OF THE SHRINE

The Basilica of St. Mary of the Immaculate Conception, located in downtown Norfolk, is the oldest parish community in the Catholic Diocese of Richmond and is often referred to as "The Mother Church of Tidewater Virginia."

The church came into existence in 1791 as St. Patrick's Church, two years before the establishment of the U.S. hierarchy and twenty-nine years before the institution of the Richmond diocese. Its first parishioners were French Catholics, compelled to abandon their native land by the French Revolution. St. Patrick's received some of the earliest Irish Catholic immigrants in the United States.

The original church was built in 1842 and was destroyed by fire in 1856, rendering the building unusable as a church. In 1858, the present church building was erected. It was dedicated to Mary of the Immaculate Conception and was the first church to bear the name after the promulgation of the dogma of the Immaculate Conception by Pope Pius IX.

African American Catholics began attending St. Mary's in 1886, where a portion of the choir loft was reserved for them. Subsequently, in 1889 the Josephites began coming from Richmond and by September of that year, St. Joseph's Black Catholic parish was founded with the Josephites serving as priests. Their mission was to serve the spiritual needs of the black community. Seventy-two years later, in 1961, St. Joseph's was merged with St. Mary's. On November 1, 1981, the newly renovated/restored edifice was rededicated with the Most Rev. Pio Laghi, apostolic pro-nuncio, the principal celebrant.

Today, St. Mary's Catholic Church is 99 percent African American. The parish supports St. Mary's Academy, an inner-city school that provides a Christian education to hundreds of urban children, most of whom are non-Catholic. The parish also operates a soup kitchen and provides other outreach to Norfolk's poor and homeless.

On December 8, 1991, the Church of St. Mary of the Immaculate Conception became a minor basilica, which coincided with the two hundredth anniversary of the church. Archbishop Agostino Cacciavillan, the apostolic pro-nuncio, read the official proclamation and was the principal celebrant of the liturgy. The basilica is an honorary title recognizing the distinguished nature of St. Mary's. There are thirty-three other minor basilicas in the United States; St. Mary's is the only one in the Commonwealth of Virginia. December 8 is the main celebration at the basilica.

SCHEDULE OF MASSES
Sunday Vigil: 5:00 p.m.
Sunday: 9:00 a.m., noon
Tuesday–Friday: 12:10 p.m.
Holy Day of Obligation: 12:10 p.m., 7:30 p.m.
Confessions: Saturday: 4:15 p.m. and upon request

DEVOTIONS
Rosary: Before Sunday Masses
Christian Initiation Program for Adults: Weekly
Christian Initiation Program for Children: Weekly
Feast of the Immaculate Conception: December 8

FACILITIES
Soup Kitchen
St. Mary's Academy: Pre-K through Fifth Grade

LANGUAGES
English and North American Sign Language

West

Shrine of St. Therese

DIOCESE OF JUNEAU
MAILING ADDRESS: 5933 LUND STREET • JUNEAU, AK 99801
LOCATED AT MILE 23 • (907) 780-6112

HISTORY OF THE SHRINE

Fr. William G. LeVasseur, SJ, had a vision of establishing a retreat center/shrine on an island along the Inside Passage, a Pacific Ocean waterway amid forested islands. With the blessing and support of Bishop Joseph Raphael Crimont, the dream began to take shape during the 1930s. With much volunteer help and through the grace of God, a stone chapel, a log retreat lodge, and smaller retreat cabins were constructed near the shrine.

The shrine was dedicated to St. Therese of Lisieux, who was chosen to be the patroness of Alaska by Bishop Crimont, the first bishop for the entire state of Alaska. St. Therese is a twentieth-century saint known for the little ways in which she reached out to God's people as a way to please her Creator and Lord. She believed that the God of Mercy had a special love for ordinary people because he created so many of them, and she considered herself among them. The message of St. Therese teaches us that no one has to earn God's love; he loves us first, and our call is to respond to and accept that love and in turn share that love.

The chapel, lodge, and cabins serve the needs of those on retreats and also provide a place of spiritual refuge and renewal for individuals, couples, families, and groups. The beauty, peace, and serenity that flow from this sacred place help individuals heal their relationships with themselves, God, and others.

SCHEDULE OF MASSES
Sunday: 1:30 p.m. (Summer)
Confessions: Upon request

DEVOTIONS
Peace Prayer Vigil: Third weekend in February
Feast of St. Therese of Lisieux: October 1
Bishop Crimont's Anniversary: May 20
Memorial Day
Retreats and Days of Recollection: Varies

FACILITIES

Retreat Lodge Center with overnight accommodations (reservations required)
Other overnight accommodations (e.g., cabins available for small retreats)
Religious Gift Shop
Cafeteria (meals are provided with lodge retreats when requested by group)
Shrine: services, weddings

OTHER ACTIVITIES

Outdoor Stations of the Cross
Fishing
Picnicking
Diving, Beachcombing
Trails
Wildlife viewing (eagles, marten, mink, whales, sea lions, salmon)

Shrine of
St. Joseph of the Mountains

P.O. BOX 267 • 16949 SHRINE ROAD • YARNELL, AZ 85362
OFF PHOENIX–PRESCOTT HIGHWAY 89
(520) 778-5229 • (520) 427-3436

HISTORY OF THE SHRINE

On July 15, 1934, a small group of lay men and women in Phoenix gathered to form an organization whose sole aim was to perform the spiritual and corporal works of mercy, regardless of race or creed. The members came from various parishes. Fr. Matin Knauff, OFM, then pastor of St. Mary's Church, was chosen as their spiritual director. This group, the Catholic Action League, while small in number, has gone quietly and steadily onward in its works of mercy and kindness.

The shrine was built with private donations in 1939, and the first pilgrimage was held the same year, on July 23. The second pilgrimage took place July 23, 1940; its theme was "For God and Country." In 1947, the shrine expanded its religious instruction by erecting the fourteen Stations of the Cross, explaining through Scripture the suffering, death, and resurrection of Jesus. Thus, the shrine became an ecumenical church outdoors with nature for its walls and surroundings.

The shrine is still staffed by volunteers and supported solely by donations and Gift Shop sales. The Shrine of St. Joseph of the Mountains promotes St. Joseph as the foster father of Jesus, head of the Holy Family, and patron and role model to the family of today.

The shrine contains life-size figures of St. Joseph with the Christ Child; Christ at the Last Supper; the Agony in the Garden; the Crucifixion; Sorrowful Mother; the Tomb; and the Risen Christ. The Stations of the Cross wind their way up and around the beautiful surrounding hills.

FACILITIES

Gift Shop, weekends 11:00 a.m.–5:00 p.m.
Clean rest rooms and public picnic area close by.

Additional Information: Yarnell Peeple's Valley Chamber of Commerce
163 Broadway Street
Yarnell, AZ 85362
Phone: (520) 427-6588

Basilica of
San Carlos Borromeo

DIOCESE OF MONTEREY
CARMEL MISSION, RIO ROAD AND LAUSEN DRIVE
P.O. BOX 2235 • CARMEL, CA 93921 • (408) 624-1271

HISTORY OF THE SHRINE

Carmel Mission stands today as a monument to Padre Junípero Serra, who left his home to come to the western wilderness in order to preach the Gospel of Christ. Padre Serra arrived by vessel at Monterey, Calif., on June 3, 1770, and founded the Mission of San Carlos. On August 24, 1771, with few provisions, he began his ministry at Carmel. Padre Serra also founded nine other missions. His frail health overtook him at age 71; he died August 28, 1784, leaving behind a thriving mission. From 1770 to 1836, more than four thousand Native Americans were baptized at Carmel.

The mission was then run by Padre Lausen, who in 1793 undertook the building of the present stone church, which had been the hope of Padre Serra. Over the next four years, the church was built on the site of the first adobe church, from native sandstone quarried from the nearby Santa Lucia Mountains. The church was dedicated in 1797.

By 1823, the Native American population had dwindled; eleven years later, Carmel was secularized. Destruction of the mission life was complete by 1836. The church gradually decayed, and it was not until 1884 that Fr. Casanova began the work of saving this historic landmark. A new era of building began in 1931, and two years later, Bishop Philip G. Scher of the diocese raised Carmel Mission to the status of parish church.

In 1960, Pope John XXIII, through the Sacred Congregation of Rites, granted Bishop Aloysius J. Willinger's petition that Carmel Mission as a historical shrine be raised to the status of minor basilica. It now stands as one of the few basilicas in the western United States.

The mission church, two museums, cemetery, and Munras Memorial are open to the public.

SCHEDULE OF MASSES
Sunday: 7:00 a.m., 8:00 a.m., 9:30 a.m., 11:00 a.m., 12:30 p.m., 5:30 p.m.
Daily: 7:00 a.m., noon, 5:30 p.m.

DEVOTIONS
Vespers: First Friday: 7:30 p.m.

FACILITIES
Museum and Gift Shop: Monday–Saturday, 9:30 a.m.–4:30 p.m.;
     Sunday, 10:30 a.m.–4:30 p.m.

Shrine of Our Lady of Sorrows

OUR LADY OF LOURDES PARISH • DIOCESE OF SACRAMENTO
MAILING ADDRESS: 745 WARE AVENUE • COLUSA, CA 95932
LOCATED IN SYCAMORE, CALIF. • (916) 458-4170

HISTORY OF THE SHRINE

The shrine is the site of the first Catholic Mass in Colusa County, Calif. in May 1856. Fr. Peter Magagnotto, a Passionist priest from Marysville, presided. In 1864, a German missionary, Fr. Lefauber, preached a mission at the site, which is located in the village of Sycamore, a few miles southeast of Colusa. As a memorial of the mission, he erected a cross, 27 feet high with a crosspiece 12 feet wide.

The idea of building a church on the Sycamore site was abandoned in favor of establishing a mission church in the county seat of Colusa. The mission was dedicated to the Immaculate Conception in 1868 and became a parish in 1870. When the present parish church was dedicated in 1880, the parish was placed under the patronage of Our Lady of Lourdes. Masses, pilgrimages, and visits continued at the Sycamore site, however, which became the property of the Diocese of Sacramento in 1883.

Later in 1883, Fr. Michael Wallrath, pastor of the parish in Colusa from 1877 to 1912, erected a small shrine containing an altar within a few feet of the wooden cross. He dedicated the shrine to Our Lady of Sorrows. He built the shrine with bricks from his own brick works. He sold bricks in order to finance the construction of the parish church. After building the church, he used the remaining bricks to erect the little shrine. In 1922, the shrine was restored by the Knights of Columbus, who replaced the orginal wooden cross with a cement one.

The shrine was placed on the National Register of Historic Places in December 1974, the first landmark in Colusa County to receive that distinction. In 1979, the shrine was restored again, this time by members of Our Lady of Lourdes Parish. The altar was painted, the crucifix was restored, and a donation box was placed on the wall. The Ten Commandments (hand lettered on slabs of the original interior stucco) were hung, and a bronze plaque was erected at the entrance. In 1996, due to repeated vandalism, security grills were installed. A new crucifix was hung, the entrance was painted, and the masonry was repaired. The site is now adorned with cypress and orange trees and is surrounded by farm land.

Visitors are invitied to take time to rest, pray, and meditate, and to attend the two annual Masses.

SCHEDULE OF MASSES

Last Sunday in April (weather permitting): 4:00 p.m. with blessing of seed.
     The Mass is followed by a picnic supper.
Thanksgiving Day Mass: 10:00 a.m. with blessing of the crops.

Cathedral of the Blessed Sacrament

DIOCESE OF SACRAMENTO
1017 11TH STREET • SACRAMENTO, CA 95814-3806 • (916) 444-3071

HISTORY OF THE SHRINE

The dedication of the Cathedral of the Blessed Sacrament on June 30, 1889, was a momentous event that marked the beginning of its first century as part of the life and witness of the Diocese of Sacramento. The cathedral's most striking feature is its European stained-glass windows. Made in Austria, the windows incorporate glass believed to have been made in the fifteenth century. The renovation of the cathedral's interior in 1971 added the rose window in the balcony and several other panels over the main doors and altar.

The cathedral bells are of special interest. Four bells in one group—the chimes, which are rung to designate the quarter hours—weigh 1,000 to 4,000 pounds each. The largest bell, which tolls the hour and weighs 8,000 pounds, was a gift of Bishop Patrick Manogue. The bell carries an inscription in Latin which translates as "Morning, noon, and evening we will sing the Praise of the Lord, of the Most Blessed Sacrament, and of St. Patrick."

There are many impressive examples of paintings in the church, the most notable is a reproduction of the *Sistine Madonna* by Raphael Sazio (1488–1520). This reproduction was made possible through diplomatic channels with the King of Saxony, who gave his permission in a letter dated February 10, 1889. Other paintings in the cathedral include: *The Archangel Michael Crushing Satan, The Holy Family, The Death of a Martyr, The Descent from the Cross, The Stations of the Cross,* and *Our Lady of Guadalupe.* The cathedral also includes statues of the Blessed Virgin, St. Joseph, St. Patrick, the Sacred Heart of Jesus, St. Therese of Lisieux, St. Anthony, St. Jude, St. Martín de Porres, and the Infant Jesus of Prague.

The Cathedral of the Blessed Sacrament is the mother church of the Diocese of Sacramento. Visitors of all faiths are welcome to drop in to see the church, to stop and meditate in quiet surroundings, and to attend one of the services. Tours can be arranged by calling the rectory secretary for an appointment.

SCHEDULE OF MASSES
Sunday Vigil: 5:00 p.m.
Sunday: 8:00 a.m., 10:00 a.m., noon, 1:30 p.m. (Spanish), 5:00 p.m.
Daily: 7:00 a.m., noon
Saturday: noon, 5:00 p.m.
Confessions: Monday–Friday, 11:30 a.m.–noon; Saturday, 4:00–4:45 p.m.

DEVOTIONS
March: St. Patrick, the patron saint of the diocese
October: Blessing of Animals in honor of St. Francis of Assisi

Mission Basilica
San Diego de Alcala

DIOCESE OF SAN DIEGO

10818 SAN DIEGO MISSION ROAD • SAN DIEGO, CA 92108-2498 • (619) 283-7319

HISTORY OF THE SHRINE

The Mission San Diego de Alcala was California's first church, founded on July 16, 1769, by Padre Junípero Serra. The mission was relocated on the site in 1774 in order to be nearer to the Indian villages, a reliable source of water, and good land for farming.

Mission San Diego became known as the Mother of the Missions that stretch through northern California. In 1775, Indians attacked the mission and destroyed it by burning the tinder-dry buildings. Padre Luis Jayme was killed in this attack when he tried to calm the Indians; he became the first Christian martyr in California and is buried in the mission sanctuary.

Padre Serra returned to the site in 1776 and began reconstruction of the church and mission buildings. This time, the padres used adobe to cover the walls and tile for the roofs, which would protect them from fire in case of future attacks. By 1780, most of the reconstruction of the mission and outbuildings was completed. The church and other buildings were arranged in a quadrangle around a patio.

In 1797, 565 Indians were baptised, which brought the number of converts to 1,405. The land area grew to 50,000 acres, including wheat, barley, corn, and beans fields, as well as vineyards, orchards, and a variety of vegetable gardens. During this time, the mission owned 20,000 sheep, 10,000 cattle, and 1,250 horses. The second church was damaged by an earthquake in 1803; the present church has a buttress-like structure, which has withstood subsequent earthquakes.

The U.S. Cavalry occupied the mission from 1846 until 1862. The soldiers made some temporary repairs to the decayed buildings in order to make them habitable. In 1862, the mission lands were restored to the church by order of President Abraham Lincoln.

Pope Paul VI named the present mission church a minor basilica in 1976. Today it serves as an active parish for the Catholic community and as a cultural center for people of all faiths, who are most welcome to visit the mission and relive the grandeur and excitement of two hundred years.

SCHEDULE OF MASSES

Sunday Vigil: 5:30 p.m.

Sunday: 7:00 a.m., 8:00 a.m., 9:00 a.m., 10:00 a.m., 11:00 a.m. (Spanish), noon (Choir), 5:30 p.m.

Daily: 7:00 a.m., 5:30 p.m.

La Mision de San Francisco de Asís

ARCHDIOCESE OF SAN FRANCISCO
3321 16TH STREET • SAN FRANCISCO, CA 94114 • (415) 621-8203

HISTORY OF THE SHRINE

The shrine—founded June 29, 1776, by Fr. Francisco Paulou, OFM, under the direction of Fr. Junípero Serra, OFM—was the sixth of the twenty-one Spanish California missions. It is considered the birthplace of the City of San Francisco. Originally the site of the evangelization of the Ohlone, Miwok, Patwin, Wappo, and Coast Miwok Indians, the shrine and basilica now serve as a parish church continuing the evangelization work of the Franciscan Missionaries. It provides spiritual life to 1,700 families within the boundaries of the parish and to its many visitors from the city and around the world. The larger church, built in 1913, was declared a basilica by Pope Pius XII in 1952.

Important events during the year include *Señor de los Milagros* in October (Peruvian), *La Purisima Concepción* in December (Nicaraguan), *Nuestra Señora de Guadalupe* in December (Mexican), and *Procesión del Santo Entierro* on Good Friday (Hispanic). The founding of the mission is celebrated annually on June 29.

SCHEDULE OF MASSES
Sunday Vigil: mission, 5:00 p.m.
Sunday: basilica, 8:00 a.m., 10:00 a.m., noon (Spanish)
Monday–Saturday: mission, 7:30 a.m.; basilica, 9:00 a.m.
Holy Day of Obligation: 7:30 a.m., 9:00 a.m., 6:00 p.m. (Bilingual)
Confessions: Saturday: 4:00–5:00 p.m.

DEVOTIONS
Rosary: Monday–Saturday, 8:40 a.m.
Adoration/Benediction: Friday, 6:00 p.m.

FACILITIES
Mission San Francisco de Asís
Gift Shop
Museum
Cemetery
Basilica of Mission Dolores

LANGUAGES
English and Spanish spoken
English, Spanish, German, Italian, and French Old Mission informational brochures

San Juan Bautista Mission

DIOCESE OF MONTEREY
P.O. BOX 400 • SECOND AND MARIPOSA STREETS • SAN JUAN BAUTISTA, CA 95045
(408) 623-2127

HISTORY OF THE SHRINE

San Juan Bautista Mission was founded in 1797 by Fr. Fermin Francisco Lausen, a Franciscan from Vitoria, Spain. It was the fifteenth mission in California and one of the nine started by Fr. Lausen. It is the largest mission, the only one with an unbroken succession of pastors since its founding, and has the only original Spanish plaza remaining in California.

In 1803, the cornerstone was laid for the present church. With three naves or aisles, it became the widest of all the mission churches. It was dedicated in 1812. Interior completion of the church continued through 1817, when the floor was tiled and the main altar and *reredos* (which holds the six statues) were completed by Thomas Doak, an American sailor who jumped ship in Monterey and who painted them in exchange for room and board.

The church was secularized in 1835, when much of the mission property was seized by the Mexican government. In 1859, the present mission bulidings and fifty-five acres were given back to the Church by federal decree of the U.S. government.

The San Andreas fault runs along the base of the hill below the cemetery. In 1906, there was a violent earthquake that shook the greater part of central California. The side walls of the church collapsed and were restored in 1976. (Vestiges of the original El Camino Real can still be seen north of the cemetery.)The original chapel and actual mission were restored as part of the bicentennial celebrations. Goals include rebuilding the guard tower where the Spanish soldiers lived and rebuilding the missing wings of the mission.

The mission fiesta, *Dia de San Juan*, is celebrated annually. *Teatro Campesino* is held in December, and Apparitions of Our Lady of Guadalupe and La Pastorella are held every other year.

SCHEDULE OF MASSES

Sunday Vigil: 5:30 p.m.
Sunday: 9:00 a.m., 11:00 a.m., 1:00 p.m. (Spanish)
Monday–Thursday: 8:00 a.m.
Friday: 5:30 p.m.
Holy Day of Obligation Vigil: 5:30 p.m.
Holy Day of Obligation: 8:30 a.m., 5:30 p.m.
Confessions: Saturday, 4:00–5:00 p.m. and before Sunday Masses

DEVOTIONS

Bible Class: Weekly

FACILITIES

Museum
Religious Bookstore
Gift Shop
Picnic Grounds

LANGUAGES

English, Spanish, Portuguese, and Italian

Mission San Luis Rey

DIOCESE OF SAN DIEGO • FRANCISCAN FRIARS
4050 MISSION AVENUE • SAN LUIS REY, CA 92068 • (619) 757-3651

Celebrating 200 Years! 1798–1998

HISTORY OF THE SHRINE

Mission San Luis Rey, established in 1798, is the eighteenth of the twenty-one California missions, founded by the Franciscans in the eighteenth and early nineteenth centuries. In 1865, after the Period of Secularization (when missions were auctioned off by the Mexican government), President Abraham Lincoln signed a deed requiring all missions to be returned to the Church in California. Reconstruction and restoration of the mission began in 1892, and today the mission is a thriving parish, tourist attraction, and retreat center.

Approximately 50,000 people visit the mission annually.

SCHEDULE OF MASSES

Sunday Vigil: 5:30 p.m. (in Old Mission Church)
Sunday: 7:00 a.m., 8:00 a.m., 10:00 a.m., noon (Spanish), 5:00 p.m.
Confessions: Saturday, 4:00–5:00 p.m.

DEVOTIONS

Retreats: Weekly
Family Spiritual Vacation

FACILITIES

Religious Bookstore/Gift Shop
Overnight Accommodations (with reservations)
Retreat Center: Call (619) 757-3659
Museum

LANGUAGES

English and Spanish

Shrine of Our Lady of Peace

DIOCESE OF SAN JOSE
2800 MISSION COLLEGE BOULEVARD • SANTA CLARA, CA 95054 • (408) 988-4585

HISTORY OF THE SHRINE

In 1976, Fr. John Sweeney, pastor of Our Lady of Peace Church in Santa Clara, Calif., commissioned noted sculptor Charles Parks to portray the Blessed Virgin Mary through a stainless steel statue. Begun in 1980, the 7,200-pound statue rises 32 feet and rests on a 12-foot landscaped mound. The head, hands, and feet are cast in stainless steel. The gown is constructed of welded strips of stainless steel.

The Shrine of Our Lady of Peace was dedicated on October 7, 1983, by Most Rev. Pierre DuMaine, bishop of San Jose. A hand-illumined papal blessing was presented to the shrine on that occasion.

The Shrine of Our Lady of Peace holds a Fatima Pilgrimage on the thirteenth day of each month, May through October, with Mass beginning at 7:30 p.m. In 1917, Mary appeared to three children in Fatima, Portugal, on those days and invited all the world to pray for peace. This pilgrimage reproduces the ceremonies celebrated at Fatima with a candlelight Rosary and Blessing of the Sick.

SCHEDULE OF MASSES

Sunday Vigil: 5:00 p.m.
Sunday: 7:30 a.m., 9:00 a.m., 10:30 a.m., noon, 5:00 p.m., 7:00 p.m.
Daily: 8:00 a.m., noon, 5:15 p.m.; also Wednesday: 7:30 p.m. and
    Saturday: 8:00 a.m.
First Friday: 8:00 a.m., noon, 5:15 p.m., 7:30 p.m.
Holy Day of Obligation Vigil: 7:30 p.m.
Holy Day of Obligation: 8:00 a.m., 9:00 a.m., noon, 5:15 p.m., 7:30 p.m.
Confessions: Saturday, 3:30–5:00 p.m., 7:30–9:00 p.m.; before all Masses; and
    upon request.

DEVOTIONS

Tuesday: 11:00 a.m. Holy Hour and celebration of the Eucharist in honor of Mary
First Friday: All-night Vigil beginning with Mass at 7:30 p.m. and concluding with
    First Saturday Mass at 5:00 a.m.
Fatima Pilgrimage: Thirteenth day of each month. Mass at 7:30 p.m.
Perpetual Adoration: The Blessed Sacrament is exposed day and night for perpetual
    adoration.

Shrine of St. Joseph, Guardian of the Redeemer

DIOCESE OF MONTEREY
OBLATES OF ST. JOSEPH—CALIFORNIA PROVINCE
544 W. CLIFF DRIVE • SANTA CRUZ, CA 95060
SHRINE: (408) 471-0442 • BOOKSTORE: (408) 471-1700 • FAX (408) 457-1317

HISTORY OF THE SHRINE

A benefactor donated a parcel of bayside property to the congregation of St. Joseph on December 8, 1949, in answer to the Oblate Fathers' fervent March novena to their patron, St. Joseph. Groundbreaking for the construction of a seminary and chapel took place on September 30, 1951. Ten months later, the first Mass was celebrated in the chapel. Bishop Aloysius J. Willinger granted permission as early as March 7, 1952, for pilgrimages to this "shrine," and blessed it on August 31, 1952, as a "semi-public oratory dedicated to St. Joseph."

From 1952 until 1992, the construction remained with the incomplete appearance of a crypt. The Oblates' dream to construct large National Shrine of St. Joseph above the crypt went unrealized for forty years. Finally in late 1992, extensive remodeling began on the chapel; it was completed in 1993. Bishop Sylvester Ryan of the Diocese of Monterey dedicated the chapel on November 3, 1993, and declared it a diocesan shrine according to the norms of canon law, with the title "Shrine of St. Joseph, Guardian of the Redeemer." The title is chosen after the name of Pope John Paul II's apostolic exhortation on St. Joseph, *Redemptoris Custos* (*Guardian of the Redeemer*). Bishop Ryan also deposited under the altar a relic of Blessed Joseph Marello, bishop of Acqui and founder of the Oblates of St. Joseph, who had been beatified on September 26, 1993.

The shrine chapel continues to serve as a place of devotion for the Oblate religious community and for individual and group pilgrims from near and far. It contains a variety of beautiful devotional artwork, the most striking of which is a 6' x 8' original Italian wood carving of St. Joseph, Husband of Mary, Guardian of Jesus, and Patron of the Church.

SCHEDULE OF MASSES

Sunday: 11:30 a.m.
Daily: 11:00 a.m.
Confessions: Daily, 30 minutes before Mass

DEVOTIONS

Novena to St. Joseph: Every Wednesday after Mass
Annual Novena of Masses to St. Joseph: March 10–18
First Fridays Adoration of the Blessed Sacrament: 11:30 a.m.–2:30 p.m.
Annual Feasts: Holy Spouses (January 23), St. Joseph (March 19),
    St. Joseph the Worker (May 1), Blessed Joseph Marello (May 30),
    Anniversary of Shrine Dedication (November 3), and Holy Family
    (Sunday in Octave of Christmas or December 30).

FACILITIES

Shrine Chapel seating about 200
Guardian of the Redeemer Bookstore, specializing in St. Joseph and Blessed Marello
    literature
St. Joseph Art Exhibit, containing nineteenth-century original retablos from New
    Mexico and contemporary religious icons
Blessed Marello Conference Room
Masante Hall

San Buenaventura Mission

ARCHDIOCESE OF LOS ANGELES
211 E. MAIN STREET • VENTURA, CA 93001 • (805) 643-4318

HISTORY OF THE SHRINE

Padre Junípero Serra raised a cross at *la playa de la canal de Santa Barbara*, the beach of the Santa Barbara Channel, on Easter morning, March 31, 1782. Assisted by Padre Pedro Benito Cambon, he celebrated a High Mass and dedicated a mission to San Buenaventura (St. Bonaventure).

Following the mission's first church building's destruction by fire, the construction of a second church was abandoned because "the door gave way." In 1792, work began on the present church and the small utility building, which formed a quadrangle enclosing a plaza. The church was completed in 1809 and was dedicated on September 9, 1809; the first liturgical services took place a day later.

In December 1976, the church was solemnly consecrated by Cardinal Timothy Manning. Six years later, the mission marked its bicentennial anniversary. The old mission welcomes visitors and pilgrims anytime.

SCHEDULE OF MASSES
Sunday Vigil: 5:30 p.m., 7:30 p.m. (Spanish)
Sunday: 7:30 a.m., 9:00 a.m., 10:30 a.m. (Spanish), noon
Daily: 7:30 a.m.
Holy Day of Obligation Vigil: 5:30 p.m.
Holy Day of Obligation: 7:30 a.m., noon, 5:30 p.m., 7:30 p.m. (Spanish)
Confessions: Saturday, 3:30–5:00 p.m.; also Monday after Devotions

DEVOTIONS
Mass and Novena to Our Lady of the Miraculous Medal: Mondays, 7:30 p.m.

FACILITIES
Gift Shop
Religious Bookstore
Mission Museum

LANGUAGES
English and Spanish

Mother Cabrini Shrine

ARCHDIOCESE OF DENVER

20189 CABRINI BOULEVARD • GOLDEN, CO 80401 • (303) 526-0758 • FAX (303) 526-9795

HISTORY OF THE SHRINE

St. Frances Xavier Cabrini established the shrine for the purpose of spreading the Gospel and of providing a peaceful summer atmosphere for orphan children.

On the site of the shrine lie large white stones that Mother Cabrini arranged in the shape of a heart, surrounded by a smaller stone cross and a crown of thorns. A 22-foot statue of the Sacred Heart stands adorned by the Stations of the Cross, the Mysteries of the Rosary, and the Ten Commandments. A cool spring of miraculous water still flows today after Mother Cabrini found it on the barren hilltop. The main celebration of the year is the annual pilgrimage in July, which always attracts a large crowd.

The Missionary Sisters of the Sacred Heart of Jesus, founded by St. Cabrini, serve and minister to the needs of the many people who visit the shrine daily, seeking comfort, solace, and the Lord's peace.

SCHEDULE OF MASSES

Sunday: 7:30 a.m., 11:00 a.m.
Holy Day of Obligation: 7:30 a.m.
Confessions: Prior to Sunday Masses

DEVOTIONS

Novenas: Annually
Retreats: Annually

FACILITIES

Overnight Accommodations
Gift Shop
Cafeteria
Museum

LANGUAGES

English and Spanish

The Shrine of the Stations of the Cross (Sangre de Cristo)

DIOCESE OF PUEBLO
P.O. BOX 326 • 511 CHURCH PLACE • SAN LUIS, CO 81152 • (719) 672-3685

HISTORY OF THE SHRINE

The Sangre de Cristo was built as an act of faith and love by the parishioners of the Sangre de Cristo Parish. It was conceived in 1986, the centennial jubilee year of the parish.

The Shrine of the Stations of the Cross is located on a mesa in the center of San Luis, Colorado's oldest town. The shrine is known formally as *La Mesa de la Piedad y de la Misericordia* (Hill of Piety and Mercy).

The Stations of the Cross are a series of graphic meditations of the last hours of Christ's life, his judgment, sufferings, and death. Christ's Resurrection is symbolized as the "Fifteenth" Station.

The trail, which is less than a mile long, culminates in a Grotto of Our Lady of Guadalupe that contains pink sandstone statues carved in Mexico of Juan Diego and the Virgin. The grotto is a reminder of the special place that Mary has in the role of salvation and of the love that Hispanics have for the Mother of God under the title of Our Lady of Guadalupe.

Meditation chapel is now finished.

SCHEDULE OF MASSES
Sunday Vigil: 7:00 p.m.
Sunday: 7:45 a.m., 10:30 a.m.
Daily: 7:00 a.m.
Holy Day of Obligation Vigil: 7:00 p.m.
Holy Day of Obligation: 7:00 a.m., 7:00 p.m.

DEVOTIONS

Novena to San Isidro: Nine days before May 15
Feast of San Isidro: May 15
Feast of San Acasio: June 15
Feast of Ss. Peter and Paul: June 28 and 29
Feast of St. James: July 25
Feast of St. Ann: July 26
Feast of St. Cajetan: August 7
Feast of Our Lady of Guadalupe: December 12
Posadas: December 16–24, 7:00 p.m. every evening

El Santuario de Chimayo

ARCHDIOCESE OF SANTA FE
THE SHRINE OF OUR LORD OF ESQUIPULAS
P.O. BOX 235 • CHIMAYO, NM 87522 • (505) 351-4889 • (505) 351-4360

HISTORY OF THE SHRINE

El Santuario was built between 1814 and 1816. The miraculous crucifix of Our Lord of Esquipulas was found about 1810. There is no written testimony concerning the apparition of Our Lord in the Chimayo area. Tradition has passed down the story from generation to generation by the people of El Potrero.

El Santuario has been called the Lourdes of America, although no one seems to know exactly how the name came about. There are testimonies that miracles have occurred. Fr. Sebastian Alvarez, in his letter to the Episcopal See of Durango, dated November 16, 1813, told of people coming from afar to seek cures for their ailments. As word spread about cures, many more faithful came in pilgrimage. El Santuario became a place of worship—a place to pray, to thank, to ask, to meditate, and to experience peace of mind and body.

The mass media began to notice the little shrine in the Sangre de Cristo mountains. Newspapers from Chicago, Denver, New York, and Los Angeles and *Time* and *Newsweek* magazines have all written about the shrine, resulting in a considerable number of requests for information. Nearly 300,000 people come to El Santuario annually, to worship the Almighty, to ask for peace, to fulfill a promise, and to feel the healing touch of God.

The shrine is open to visitors daily, 9:00 a.m.–5:00 p.m., June–September, and 9:00 a.m.–4:00 p.m., October–May.

SCHEDULE OF MASSES
Sunday: noon
Daily: 11:00 a.m.

FACILITIES
Gift Shop

LANGUAGES
English and Spanish

Shrine and Parish of Our Lady of Guadalupe

DIOCESE OF LAS CRUCES

P.O. BOX 296 • 3600 PARROQUIA STREET • MESILLA PARK, NM 88047 • (505) 526-8171

HISTORY OF THE SHRINE

Descendants of Tigua and Piro Indians, who had settled in this area in 1849, held an annual fiesta and dances in honor of Our Lady of Guadalupe in the city of Las Cruces, N.M., until 1910, when they were refused permission to continue their cultural practices. This led the Indians to build a small chapel on their own lands to the south of Las Cruces.

In 1914, the chapel and surrounding land were deeded to the Catholic Church with the condition that the Indians would be permitted their cultural practices and annual fiesta in honor of Our Lady of Guadalupe. In 1917, a resident priest was assigned to the pueblo, and the shrine was given parochial status. In 1921, the present adobe church was completed as an enlargement of the original chapel.

The annual fiesta begins on the evening of December 10 with a night watch (*velorio*); December 11 is a day of pilgrimage to *Tortugas* mountain; December 12 is observed with Mass and Indian dances at the shrine, rosary, benediction of the Blessed Sacrament, and a procession through the streets of the village.

The public is invited to take part in all activities December 10–12.

SCHEDULE OF MASSES

Sunday Vigil: 6:30 p.m.
Sunday: 7:30 a.m. (English), 9:00 a.m. (Spanish), 10:30 a.m. (English)
Holy Day of Obligation: 8:00 a.m., 6:30 p.m.
Confessions: Saturday, 4:00 p.m., 7:15 p.m., and upon request

DEVOTIONS

Rosary: Twelfth day of each month at *La Capilla*
Palm Sunday: Blessing of *ramos*
Feast of St. John: Sunday nearest June 24

FACILITIES

Indian dining room serves free meals December 12, noon–3:00 p.m.

LANGUAGES

English and Spanish

Our Lady of the Rosary Shrine

ARCHDIOCESE OF SANTA FE
ST. FRANCIS CATHEDRAL • THE LADY CHAPEL OF THE CATHEDRAL • SANTA FE, NM 87501
(505) 982-5619

HISTORY OF THE SHRINE

On January 24, 1625, a Hispanic community in Santa Fe received a statue of Our Lady of the Rosary, carved in Spain in the sixteenth century. The 28-inch statue, hand-carved of willow wood and standing tall, became an object of admiration to the Spanish colonists and Indians visiting Santa Fe and was called *La Conquistadora*, Our Lady of Conquering Love of All.

During the Indian rebellion in 1680, colonists took the statue to El Paso de Norte. In 1693, Don Diego de Vargas returned it to Santa Fe. He made a solemn vow of eternal remembrance, after the peaceful reconquest of Santa Fe from the Indians. In 1694, the colonists began an annual thanksgiving observance by taking *La Conquistadora* from her parish shrine to the encampment site where they had prayed to her for victory. The statue is still carried in procession annually through the streets of Santa Fe to Rosario Chapel. It then remains at the chapel for one week, at which time Novena Masses are offered daily.

Pope John XXIII ordered the papal coronation of the image in 1960. For nearly 375 years, Our Lady has helped families in the area to preserve their faith through active confraternity. The confraternity unites thousands of descendants of the Christians of Santa Fe and New Mexico. *La Cofradia*, as it is called in Spanish, celebrates fifty-five Marian Masses and feasts in the Hispanic Catholic tradition.

The main celebrations of the year are the Double Sunday Processions and Double Novena of Masses of Thanksgiving to Our Lady. The Franciscan Order staffs the shrine.

SCHEDULE OF MASSES
Sunday Vigil: 5:15 p.m.
Sunday: 6:00 a.m., 8:00 a.m. (Spanish), 10:00 a.m., noon, and 7:00 p.m.
Holy Day of Obligation Masses follow Sunday schedule.
Confessions: Monday–Saturday, 3:00–5:00 p.m.

NOVENA
Sunday after Corpus Christi

LANGUAGES
English, Spanish, and Native American languages

National Sanctuary of Our Sorrowful Mother— The Grotto

ARCHDIOCESE OF PORTLAND IN OREGON
NE 85TH AVENUE AND SANDY BOULEVARD • P.O. BOX 20008 • PORTLAND, OR 97294-0008
(503) 254-7371

HISTORY OF THE SHRINE

Servite Fr. Ambrose Mayer, OSM (originally of Kitchener, Ontario, Canada) founded the shrine as an act of gratitude to God for an answer to a prayer for his mother. She was close to death as a result of childbirth. Fr. Mayer, a boy at the time, promised to do something great for God if his mother survived.

Established in 1924 and staffed by the Order of the Servants of Mary, The Grotto (The National Sanctuary of Our Sorrowful Mother) encompasses sixty-two acres of gardens, shrines, meditative pathways and ponds on two levels. Approximately 150,000 visitors and pilgrims seek out this holy shrine and natural gallery in the woods annually. Tour and pilgrimage groups make The Grotto a special destination.

SCHEDULE OF MASSES
Sunday: 10:00 a.m. (and noon, May–October, outdoors)
Daily: noon
Saturday: 8:00 a.m.
Holy Day of Obligation: Call for times
Confessions: By appointment

DEVOTIONS
St. Peregrine Mass with anointing: noon, First Saturday of each month
Freedom Day Celebration sponsored by the Southeast Asian Vicariate,
    Archdiocese of Portland: July.
Festival of Lights Christmas Celebration: December

FACILITIES
Counseling Center
Welcome Center
Gift Shop
Coffee Express
Visitor Complex
Meeting Rooms
Private Retreats
Chapel of Mary
Gardens and Shrines
Cliffside Meditation Chapel

Index

SHRINES AND PLACES DEDICATED TO THE MYSTERY OF CHRIST

SHRINES AND PLACES DEDICATED TO THE BLESSED MOTHER

SHRINES AND PLACES DEDICATED TO THE SAINTS